HOW TO LOVE
AND SURVIVE YOUR
TEENAGE DOG

BARBARA HODEL

HOW TO
LOVE
AND SURVIVE
YOUR
TEENAGE
DOG

A catalogue record for this
book is available from the
National Library of Australia

Hodel, Barbara (author)
How to Love and Survive Your Teenage Dog
ISBN 978-1-922337-56-6 (paperback)
978-1-922452-05-4 (ebook)
PETS / DOGS / TRAINING

Edited by Rebecca Hendershott
Cover photo by Ueli Schmied
Cover and book design by Green Hill Publishing

DISCLAIMER
The information in this book is written
to be used as guidance only. Outcomes
will differ due to variables including
pet history, practice and delivery.

Dedication

To our dogs, the ones we have lost but who are still in our hearts and the ones who are with us – Shellbe and Chillax – who make everyday fun and, sometimes, challenging.

Table of Contents

Table of Contents

Table of Contents

Chapter 1
Don't feel bad –
And keep it positive!

Are you living with a young dog? Then you can probably relate to your dog being spooked by a man with a hat, disappearing in the distance chasing a rabbit, coming home to a loungeroom filled with white fluff or a dug-up back yard. The puppy has become a teenager – and it happened almost overnight – just when you thought all was going well!

As with humans, dogs need to go through the teenage phase to reach the stability of adulthood and there are biological reasons for a lot of the frustrating behaviours we see in teenage dogs. Understanding those reasons will help us in dealing with these challenges. To put it simply, during the adolescent period the brain is still under construction. Different parts of the brain mature at different rates and teenage dogs have a hard time making good decisions, exhibiting self-control, remembering their training and they are hyper-emotional.

As parents of teenage humans can undoubtedly relate to, sometimes doggy teenagehood becomes too much and we reach our wit's end and are not sure if we are going to make it. Sometimes we feel discouraged and down because we thought we had done everything right when they were puppies, but it doesn't seem to be enough. Often, we are ill-prepared for the challenges of a teenage dog. The emotional responses and over-the-top reactions to some stimuli, forgotten training, increased exercise and mental-stimulation requirements and the need for ongoing socialisation and training can take us by surprise. There are days when they rush up barking at a stranger and days when everything scares them. We become disappointed or are tempted to give up.

Most dogs are lucky enough to come out of this challenging time with the relationship intact and a bright future ahead. Unfortunately, some dogs do not make it to the end of their teenage months. They may end up in the pound, foster homes or even euthanised at an early age. Because of their challenging behaviours some end up in the backyard spending their lives lonely and bored, never reaching their full potential or being happy and content. This need not happen to our canine companions, as long as we have patience, clear communication and understand their point of view.

Teenagehood is a normal development stage and does not mean we failed at training. The challenges for this life stage are as predictable as the challenges for puppyhood, although the solutions are not

Shellbe and Chillax at the coffee shop. Well-trained and socialised dogs can go places and share more of their lives with us. That's what I want with my dogs and hopefully you do, too! Picture Barbara Hodel.

as straightforward. With puppies we are mostly dealing with house-training, mouthing, exuberance, being home alone, the 'witching hours' and early socialisation. Small dogs, small problems. The challenges with teenage dogs are more complex and can go to the core of our relationship with our dogs. Some of the teenage behaviours are so testing that we feel that our relationship is at stake. We also might find our teenage dog, who does not follow expected social norms, is not an acceptable member of our society and therefore feel that we have failed.

A teenage dog who has started fighting at the dog park may become a liability, a dog who has forgotten their recall might put themselves and others at risk, a dog who gets scared of strangers and barks and lunges might be considered aggressive. These problems are testing for any relationship and even more so for unprepared humans. Don't give up. It does not have to be like this. You can get your teenage dog and your relationship back on track!

Overall, the teenage months are a challenging time for most dogs and their humans. It is also a time when some dogs are surrendered because we cannot deal with their emotional responses. Surprisingly, while there are countless articles and books on puppy raising, there is significantly less information available once the cute puppy becomes a 'stroppy' teenager; how to deal with the challenging teenage dog is where this book comes in. Dog-training is a team effort and both dogs and humans need to learn, understand, trust each other and communicate effectively to reach their full potential and create a relationship that stands the test of time. Only if we teach both humans and dogs with science-based, humane and ethical training methods can we transform lives and make the world a better place for dogs and humans. This book can help you achieve a fulfilling relationship with your dog based on trust and mutual understanding.

So, do you find your teenage dog challenging? Don't feel bad! This book is for you! You will learn how to survive your dog's teenage period without reverting to punishment, which can jeopardise your relationship and the wellbeing of all involved. Positive reinforcement training has been proven to work best for dogs and humans alike and with the least side effects. Keeping it positive is better for your relationship with your dogs and will lead to much better results. This book will guide you through the challenges of the teenage phase, help you maintain a positive attitude and provide you and your dog with guidance. Remember: your teenage dog is not *giving you* a hard time; they are *having* a hard time! You are not alone and *you and your dog can do it!*

Chapter 2
Teenage dogs – Their brain is still under construction

2.1 Teenage dogs – Who are they?

All seems to be going well – house training is complete, our dog seems calmer and sleeps ok, training is going well – and then they hit the teenage phase. We were lulled into a false sense of security just before the teenage months started. The previously attentive puppy – who was doing so well with training, who was the star at puppy pre-school and who thought their human was the centre of the universe – discovers an entirely new world out there. To those who are parents of [human] teenagers, this may sound familiar.

In a human context, a teenager is defined as someone who is between being an immature child and a fully-developed adult (roughly 13-19 years of age) and is going through biological changes associated with sexual maturation. Usually physiological growth (height, weight and reproductive abilities) is complete midway through adolescence. If we apply this concept to dogs, most dogs enter this teenage stage around six to ten months and – depending on breed and size – they will finish adolescence around 12-24 months. Some dogs, for example the large gundogs, may develop slower and will be older when they end adolescence. Once they finish teenagehood, dogs have reached maturity: physically and sexually. Hopefully, they also have reached stability in their emotional reactions, behaviour and attitude towards others and life in general.

While a puppy's world revolves around their human, teenage dogs will explore, test boundaries and become more independent. They can also be moody, unpredictable, lack concentration and focus and are generally a bit of a pain (human parents: sound familiar?). In these teenage months they are finding their own identity and their place in life. As with humans, they are trying to figure out how to fit in and what works and what doesn't work. They are also becoming more adventurous, and the world becomes a place of new and exciting things, experiences and, of course, smells.

2.2 Their brain – and identity – is still under construction

While dogs are not humans and there is no science on the teenage dog brain, we can be reasonably sure that the development of the brain works very similar in humans and dogs. This is because although the teenage dog brain has not been explicitly researched, some parallels can be drawn based on the information we do have on the adult brain and behavioural observations.

A lot of research has been done on adult dog and adult human minds, and this indicates that both species' brains are relatively similarly structured. Research into adult human and teenage human minds indicate that there are developmental differences in brain structure between the age groups. Therefore, it is logical to assume that teenage dog brains differ from adult dog brains similar to how teenage human brains differ from adult human brains.

2.2.1 Adults: Dog vs. human brains

Brain structure is similar between adult dogs and humans. The main differences between the human and dog brain are that the dog's brain is (understandably) smaller in size, with less folds, a thinner cerebral cortex and relatively smaller frontal lobes[1]. The front lobes play an important role in planning and decision making, which means dogs have limited abilities in this area compared to humans. Berns, a researcher of dog brains (Emory University), points out that dogs have only a small part in their brain that regulates self-control compared to humans – even when grown-up: 'Whatever amount of self-control they have must be eked out of a small piece of brain real estate'[2]. Dogs live in the here-and-now and do not dwell on the future. It also means that the way they make decisions is more spontaneous and not based on careful planning but, rather, instant gratification. On the positive side this also means they are not plotting against us and planning on taking over the household – and then the world!

Despite these differences, it seems that dogs and humans process information in a similar way. For example, we both have similar brain regions activated by vocal stimuli, facial recognition and inhibition. In their review article *Why Did the Dog Walk into the MRI*, Berns and Cook say that dogs, similar to humans, show positive striatal response (the striatum is a brain region linked to the reward system) to the expectation of a reward[3]. This means that teaching dogs or humans should follow the same humane principles, since both love rewards (or reinforcers) and, therefore, both benefit from positive reinforcement training.

Ultimately, our deep-level co-created evolutionary relationship with dogs is reflected in how their brain has been restructured to process a human-centred lifestyle. Unlike many other species, dogs solve problems similar to humans, and they communicate, and understand humans, using eye gaze, eyebrows or pointing, as do humans[4]. Hecht, a neuroscientist (Harvard University), found that we have not only altered canine appearance but also their brain structure[5].

2.2.2 Humans: Adult vs. teenage brains

In humans, the teenage phase is associated with the most dramatic growth spurt in the brain after infancy. The teenager develops new thinking skills, which ultimately become the decision-making skills of adults. At this stage, these thinking skills are still influenced by emotions that override the rational. The more basic (or evolutionarily basal) functions at the back of the brain mature first (including emotional response). The component responsible for controlling impulse and planning – the front part – matures later, and the prefrontal cortex is remodelled last[6]. Thus, teenagers face a challenge in that the brakes develop later than the accelerators.

The risk-taking of teenagers – and the associated parental heart attacks – is a classic example of the brain not processing information correctly. There are good reasons why we only allow older teenagers to learn how to drive and get a drivers' licence. However, the way some of the P-platers drive (and research into crashes[7]) indicates that this teenage developing-brain stage is still too early to handle the complexity of driving rules, safety and awareness. In adults, the various parts of the brain work together to assess situations, evaluate choices, make decisions and then act accordingly. The teenage brain does not work as smoothly.

The intense emotions shown during teenagehood are associated with the changes in the limbic system. The limbic system is responsible for the experience and expression of emotions. This part of the brain develops before the parts that are supposed to control these emotions. This means that emotional responses, especially the urgency and intensity of the emotional reaction, are affected during this time. Because the frontal part of the brain is still developing, teenagers rely on the limbic system for their reactions. Depending on the part of the brain that is associated with impulse, aggression and instincts do not make for well-planned and calm decision-making.

Also at work during this time is a 'use it or lose it' principle: some neural connections are weakened and some are strengthened. There is a plethora of growth in synapses and a culling of unused ones, in order to make the system more efficient. This is called plasticity. But because this process starts at the back of the brain, the vital part of control – the prefrontal cortex – is the last to be trimmed. This means the prefrontal cortex in teenagers is immature compared to adults. This might be the reason that adults are better wired to notice mistakes in the decision-making process[8].

Another change in teenage bodies is the development of receptors for oxytocin, often described as the bonding hormone. This new development could explain the need for reassurance and connection despite the independence teenagers try to show. To put it simply: the teenage brain is still under construction, and the different parts are not communicating correctly with each other, making teenagers more impulsive, more emotionally-reactive and more prone to taking risks.

2.2.3 Dogs: Adult vs. teenage brains

Therefore, for the time being, I assume (until we have better research) that brain development in young dogs is similar to human teenagers because the behaviours we see in teenage dogs are very similar to those we see in teenage humans[9]: 'They are dramatic, irrational and scream for seemingly no reason. And they have a deep need for both greater independence and tender loving care.'

Teenage dogs are unable to process information like mature dogs, and often engage in risky behaviours. The risk-taking during this time is caused by the frontal cortex not registering the risk or curbing the impulse but responding only to the strong urge for an immediate reward. This is exemplified by the chase of a rabbit across a busy street without even seeing the cars. In hunting breeds this behaviour is more accentuated by their breed-specific traits.

Ultimately, we can assume, based on adult dog and adult human brain comparisons, that 'self-control' is not high on the agenda for any dog. Based on human developmental changes in the brain, we can also assume that teenage dogs have even less self-control and greater emotional reactivity, than adult dogs. As with this human research, I conclude that these hormonal needs for immediate rewards and gratification are more pronounced in teenage dogs than puppies or adults.

 In real life This issue of emotional reactivity and lack of self-control can be clearly seen when an adult dog gets spooked but then realises that the scary thing is just a human with a strange looking hat. They will adjust and walk off. Teenage dogs often are incapable of understanding the mistake and just keep barking or lunging. The developmental stage of the brain explains the seemingly irrational behaviour of the teenage dog. They do not have the brain development to make the correct assessment of the situation. They rely on the limbic system instead of the prefrontal cortex to make a decision which means an emotional over-the-top reaction instead of a calm assessment of the situation.

2.2.4 Sex differences

There also appear to be sex differences – in both humans and dogs – in risky behaviours during the teenage phase. This may be the result of sex-specific hormonal surges and initial mate-seeking/reproductive behaviours that are happening around the age of sexual maturation.

Simply, males take more risks than females. For example, teenage human males are overrepresented in driving accidents[10]. And, after more than 15 years of helping thousands of clients with their teenage dogs and bringing up both male and female dogs myself, I find that male teenage dogs are more challenging than females (in terms of increased independence, higher activity levels and lack of self-control). An article by Starling and colleagues seems to support my anecdotal evidence, by saying that male dogs are bolder than females and that younger dogs are bolder than older dogs[11]. Boldness is described as willingness to play with humans and other dogs and less avoidance behaviours indicating fear – or, in other words, risk-taking.

2.2.5 Social relationships: Teenage vs. adult

Both male and female dogs become more selective about who they consider friends as they age, and inter-dog aggression might become an issue. This is a bit like humans growing up. Children will interact and play with most other children they meet. Teens will still make new friends, and associate with different groups of friends and figure out which ones suit them best, but they will be more selective about whom they associate with than children. Once we reach adulthood, we become even more selective; we will still make new friends but not as easily as we used to. We become much more careful and will not just talk to anyone we meet at the pub or at the coffee shop. In our fifties, we are often set in our ways and socialise with our friends and family and rarely venture out to make new friends. I do not mean to imply that friendships cannot be developed in older individuals, but it is much less common than when we were younger.

The very same applies for dogs. Puppies love to play with most other puppies they meet. Teenage dogs often still love a romp at the park with new-found friends but the older they become, the more selective they are. They will prefer to play with their friends rather than complete strangers. There are some dogs, like people, who will make friends for their entire life, but they are the exception rather than the rule.

In real life I have a good friend who is in his 40s. Contrary to most other friends in that age group, he still talks to pretty much anyone he meets, makes new friends easily and is generally a very social person. I call him the Labrador. Labradors seems to be a breed that stays puppy-like in their interactions for much of their lives. This might be a side-effect of breeding for an extremely friendly family dog.

I like the way one article describes this development[12]: most dogs will start out as *dog-friendly* (playing and having fun with most dogs they meet) – these are the typical puppies and some teenage dogs will fit in here, too. From there they move on to being *dog-tolerant*. They get along with most dogs either actively playing or ignoring them. They have a rather long fuse, are tolerant of other dogs trying to play or even hump or chase. They have excellent communication skills. This is the group a lot of dogs will end up in as adults. This is also the group where we find a lot of teenage dogs. But, as they mature, they might alternatively become *dog-selective*. This means they get along only with some dogs and need guidance navigating new dog introductions. The dog-selective group is another group where a lot of dogs will end up once they reach social maturity. They will require being managed at the dog park and matched with suitable play mates if they want to play. Some dogs will become *dog-aggressive* and will require a lot of management and the dog park might not be a good place for them.

2.3 Selective hearing and forgotten training

A puppy's world revolves around their humans, and they are often reluctant to venture too far from home. They might not enjoy their walks and prefer to go home as soon as possible. A common complaint about puppies on walks is that they just sit down and refuse to move. This is very common as puppies are 'hypersensitive'; this means they feel the heat and the cold much more than adult dogs. They are also easily overwhelmed by unfamiliar sounds and sights. A puppy sitting down and trying to process the information is not stubborn but is, in fact, trying to make sense of the wider world. They are also very attached to their human and the world beyond is of little interest to them. This is normal, but it is also normal that many things change as puppies become a bit older.

Once teenage dogs realise that there is a world beyond their immediate family and home, they will become more interested in the outside world. At this stage they also have gotten used to their environment and their puppy hypersensitivity has disappeared. Their brain changes and exploration (or boldness) becomes very important. They want to explore every scent and sight and they *know* there has to be something significant around the next corner. They are so intent on exploring that it seems that they are deaf. In most cases, the issue is not that they are deaf, but their sense of smell is overriding all other senses, and they really *cannot* hear us calling.

It is a bit like us if we are engrossed in an excellent book or a TV show and we just cannot hear the husband asking for help with the dishes. Our attention is simply somewhere else. Similarly, teenage dogs have not *lost* focus, but they have *shifted* focus to something else. They are trying to process so much information that they cannot hear us.

All of this means that the teenage dogs are also having a hard time concentrating. Cues that were previously followed are met with a questioning look. They behave as if they had never heard the word *sit* and seem to have no idea what they should do when asked. The brain is not processing the information correctly as other details and impressions are overriding the human cues. The information is not lost – it is still there – but our teenage dogs cannot access it. It is critical to keep in mind that they are not purposely doing this to annoy us. They really cannot help it. They are not stubborn or stupid; they are just dealing with a brain where not all the parts have connected yet.

In real life I walked into the pet shop with my ten-month-old German short-haired pointer Chillax and he could not believe it. The smells, the sights, the other people and dogs. There was complete information overload for his developing brain. The interesting thing is that he had been to that same pet shop before and had no problems following cues. This time he had to sniff, say *hello* to everyone, explore every single shelf. He barely registered that I was there. I gave him a few minutes and in time he was able to focus. At this age, they are still learning and sometimes they just cannot make sense of what is going on. I went to the same pet shop a few months later and there was no problem at all.

2.4 Secondary fear phases

Another common problem for teenage dogs are fear phases. This is when many sociable dogs become a little nervous as they emerge from puppyhood and enter a teenage fear period[13]. Fear phases are well-documented in puppies but less so in teenage dog. The fear phase puppies go through around the eight-week mark is called the *primary fear phase*. Teenage dogs then go through several additional fear phases which are called *secondary fear phases*. Like most other aspects of teenage dogs, the secondary fear phase is not well-researched. Based on my experience, fear phases come and go throughout the teenage months. They may last for a couple weeks, go away and then reappear a few months later until the dog has reached the stability of adulthood. These fear phases are normal and temporary. As with many things during these challenging months, they seem to come back just when we thought we have seen the light at the end of the tunnel.

During these fear phases teenage dogs can become surprisingly fearful of new people and new things. Suddenly, things that used to be ignored or acknowledged with a casual glance become scary and our teenage dog barks and lunges to scare the frightening thing away. Inanimate objects (backpacks on the ground, plastic bags, wheelie bins) or 'strange' looking humans (with hats, high visibility vests, dark sunglasses, facial hair) are prime suspects for being out there to get them. This will happen with even the best-socialised puppies. However, for an under-socialised dog it is much more prevalent. The episodes are more extended and there are more things they fear. A well-socialised dog will recover more quickly from a scare because they have learned through positive exposure and repetitions that the world is a safe place.

2.5 Summary

The brains of our teenage dogs are under construction and because the front part of the brain that is responsible for controlling emotions matures last, we see them reacting in seemingly irrational ways. This brain development is also responsible for their selective hearing, 'forgotten' training and getting spooked by random people and things during fear phases. This is normal and has physiological reasons. Knowing the physiological reason behind these challenges should make it easier for us to be patient and understanding of the hard time our teenage dogs are going through.

Chapter 3
The relationship matters – Co-being between dogs and humans

There are many reasons to get dogs. We get them for company, to become more active or because puppies are cute. Or we might get them for the children, to feel safe at home, because the neighbours got one or we want to start a dog sport. When getting a dog, we all hope for this unique relationship with them; the dog who only has eyes for us, comes back every time they are called and is just a joy to live with. However, when focusing on our own reasons for wanting a dog, sometimes we do not stop and carefully assess what the dog wants and what would make them happy. Dogs love company, fun, play, games, a nice bed, good food; they love to move and have some control over the outcome of their actions. They really are very similar to humans – as are other animals.

However, we tend to forget that dogs perceive the world differently to us and this can be a challenge to our relationship. They see – or, rather, smell – different things to what we humans do. They consider things in the environment to be important that we don't give a second thought to, such as grass to roll in, critters to chase or the wee of another dog. What we consider important is often completely irrelevant to our dogs. Who cares about traffic lights, pedestrian crossing, the TV or off-limit comfortable sleeping places? Certainly not our dogs! So, while they need to live in our world (and therefore it is important to teach them how to behave in this world), it is also important to try to see the world from their perspective. This creates room for reasonable allowances, so our dogs can be part of and feel happy in their own world and not only have to comply with the rules of our world. This comes about by building a strong and respectful relationship that includes two-way communication.

Ultimately, the teenage months can become a testing time for our relationship with our young dog – not only because the cute puppy phase is history or because the children have lost interest, but because we did not anticipate the amount of time we need to spend with them. Thus, our dog's teenagehood can break down or seriously compromise our relationship with them. Fortunately, we all know that good relationships are no coincidence. They are the product of hard work and commitment. Relationships require even more work with our teenage dogs when they lack impulse control, cannot make calm decisions and want to be independent and loved at the same time. Although it is work to build a relationship with our dogs, the payback on our efforts make it worth it.

3.1 Considering dogs as friends or family

In her book *The Companion Species Manifesto*, Haraway (University of California, Santa Cruz) talks about our relationship with dogs being 'thick and messy'– it isn't all good, and it isn't all bad, but rather it is 'about meeting the other in all the fleshy detail of a mortal relationship' with all its 'inevitable comic and tragic mistakes' that occur in the 'permanent search for knowledge of the intimate other'[14]. This means we need to accept our dogs for who they are and appreciate their positives and negatives as a whole – just like what we do with friends and family. Sometimes we may not want to be around them and sometimes they may not want to be around us. They are allowed to think for themselves and do not have to perform just because we want them to. They do not exist for our needs and they have their own personal goals and preferences.

It is for this reason that I avoid terms such as 'fur baby' that indicate dependency and fail to acknowledge that dogs are independent beings with their own feelings, personalities and needs. It is understandable why some people think of their dogs as children (they are dependent on us, after all), but I would encourage people to consider dogs as beings with their own goals, voice and autonomy – as friends and family members, rather than something to own, dominate and infantilise. Haraway[15] supports this when she says

> 'I resist being called the "mom" to my dogs because I fear infantiliza-tion of the adult canines and misidentification that I wanted dogs, not babies. My multi-species family is not about surrogacy and substi-tutes; we are trying to live other tropes, other metaplasms.'

3.1.1 Mutual interspecies relationships

Part of building up a relationship is to identify where dogs socially fit into our lives. No matter the life stage, I recommend considering our dog as someone that we can share our life with, but who also have their own lives and goals and motivations – just like independent yet interde-pendent friends or family. For example, Miklósi says[16]:

> '... respecting a dog as a friend is perhaps the best approach to the human–canine relationship. Friends can be attached to each other for all their lives but they are also able to lead independent lives for a shorter or longer time... They help each other but do not expect immediate return of favors. Friends enjoy being together just for the sake of it, but they also respect one another allowing each other to develop independent personalities.'

Safina makes a similar point when he says: 'I used to think it silly for people to speak of dogs as "family" or other animals as "friends". Now I feel it is silly not to'[17].

Another aspect of having a mutual friendship with dogs is the recognition that while we think of us training dogs, dogs train us too. I do not have a problem with that; I think mutual training makes for a good relationship. For example, we may train our dog not to wee inside, while at the same time our dog is training us to let them out when they sit by the door (a 'mand behaviour'; see Section 3.2.4). By reconsidering the power and dominance associated with training – and refocusing on training as a mutual process of learning to live and communicate together – then we truly are on the path to a shared friendship and respect.

There are 'friendship-based' approaches that take 'training' and living with our dogs to a completely new level. Arnold, the founder of Canine Assistants and author of *Through a Dog's Eyes*, writes about *bond-based teaching* for training canine assistants in her book *Love Is All You Need*[18]. This approach does not 'train' dogs in a traditional way but, rather, teaches them by making them part of our social group, which in turn then influences their behaviour. By providing secure attachment, our dogs are given guidance and confidence. This method focuses on teaching the dogs to manage their own behaviour rather than merely responding to cues. It is much easier to live with a dog who understands appropriate behaviour than a dog who has to be directed constantly. What an interesting thought!

Concept training is a similar approach. *Concept training* does not teach specific behaviours but works with broad concepts such as calmness, focus and confidence to enable the dog to make the right choices for themselves in different situations. If you are interested in this approach, check out Mitchell's book *How to Be a Concept Trainer*[19]. Concept training gives more autonomy to our dogs and is based on the premises that the teaching process is cooperative. Dogs are allowed to make decisions and they have choice (see Section 3.2.4).

3.1.2 Historical relationships and outdated perceptions of dominance

Considering dogs as friends or family and treating them as such is completely different from the traditional dog-training approach. It is a different mindset for us and our dogs. Historically, our relationship with dogs was defined by control, dominance and coercion. We used *commands* and choice was an unknown concept. For humans, an unhealthy relationship is defined as a relationship 'based on power and control and not equality and respect'[20]. This sounds a lot like the traditional human–dog relationship!

The common narrative says that because dogs are pack animals with an alpha at the top of the hierarchy, the way to control dogs who try to assert dominance (by resisting what we are asking them to do) is to use punishment to 'put them into their place' and assume the role of the pack leader. While this narrative gives us humans structure and a way to deal with our dogs, it also provides a justification for using punishment and ignores more up-to-date behavioural evidence.

This outdated idea is based on studies of captive wolf behaviour where unrelated wolves were forced to live together in often cramped conditions. However, 'packs' of wolves in the wild are nothing more than a family unit with a breeding pair and their offspring, who cooperate to live together:

> 'They are families, not groups of peers vying for the top spot. [...] Behaviors seen as "dominant" or "submissive" are used not in a scramble for power, they are used to maintain social unity'[21].

'Social unity' is a very different way of thinking of wolf packs and dominance! Even more on-point, is the fact that free-ranging dogs in developing countries are the closest relatives to our pet dogs (not wolves) and they are not pack animals – they are social animals who live in loose association with each other and do not form strict linear hierarchies.

This means it is not necessary to show our dog 'who is boss' by forcefully punishing them – instead we need to find a way to 'maintain social unity'.

Ultimately, it is time that we put the notion that our dogs need to view us as their pack alpha to bed. Unfortunately, it seems that some people just cannot let go of this idea and its associated talk about alphas, dominance and submission. Fortunately, the outdated construct of packs and dominance has been replaced with more accurate information on dog social behaviour[22].

 In real life There is another very scary reason for this outdated idea still being used and propagated. The dog training industry is an unregulated industry and anyone can call themselves a 'dog trainer' – and they do. Individuals without formal education and training and no association with a professional organisation keep using this outdated construct to justify their dominance and punishment-based methods; they have not bothered to consider the more updated and science-based training techniques. I know of many well-meaning humans seeking advice from 'professionals' only to be taught to use these methods to the detriment of their dogs and themselves. Sometimes the side-effects are irreversible and lasting damage has been done to the dogs, their humans and their relationship.

3.1.3 A shift in language

A different way of interacting with our dog will also include a change in the language we use. A *command* is a threat to the dog to either do what they are told or they will be made to do it. A *cue*, on the other hand, is an opportunity to get a reinforcer. The idea of using the word *cue* instead of *command* has been around for a while (I saw it used most recently by

Sdao at the 2019 PPG Summit in Australia). Think about it: would you like to be asked to do something, or told to do something?

The same influence of language is seen in what we call the human part in this relationship. I will use *human* instead of *owner* as I think dogs are much more than owned property, despite this being our dogs' legal status. To say that 'we have a dog' is to equally acknowledge that 'our dog has us'. For example, there are large differences between people who identify as 'owners' or 'guardians' of their dogs. 'Guardians' are more likely, than 'owners', to adopt, take in strays, spay/neuter, register their dogs and make sure they have IDs, allow their dogs inside, give gifts and show affection, consider their dogs as family members, are attached and feel that pets are sentient beings and not possessions[23]. In contrast, people who label themselves 'owners' are more likely to purchase/breed dogs, lose and relinquish their dogs, view their dogs as property and feel that people shouldn't make such a big deal out of protecting animals.

Language is very powerful and it matters what words we use. While our dogs probably don't care what we call the signals we give them or the words we use to describe ourselves, they probably are aware of the difference between us 'asking nicely' or threatening punishment. It also changes our mindset and affects the way we interact with our dogs and what we expect them to do – as seen in the differences between people who identify as guardians versus owners.

3.2 Relationship ingredients

As with human relationships, there are no *recipes* for a good relationship, but there are *ingredients* that make for a good relationship. These include taking time for each other, having realistic expectations, listening to each other and communicating, showing respect, fostering mutual trust and allowing some degree of choice about daily life. All relationships need work; there are no relationships that are always just good. Actually, most are 'thick and messy'. When things are difficult and our teenage dog ignores us, we should not take it personally! It is just part of them growing up and figuring out what works and what does not work.

3.2.1 Creating relationships over time

One of the main things is that we need to make time; time to spend together and, sometimes, apart. The time we spend together should be quality time where we enjoy activities such as walking, going to the beach, training, participating in a dog sport, playing (games). Walking with the dog while talking to friends on the phone or checking social media does not count, as we are not truly present in the moment with our dog.

Most dogs need much more time than what we humans anticipate. For a teenage dog, two to three hours of quality time a day is the minimum. This does not include the time they spend with us in front of the TV or computer. While that might seem like a lot, it is the reality for an active dog.

In addition to quality time together, dogs also need to be part of the family and have access to the living areas where we spend most of our time. This 'down time' is critical to bonding, communication and building a relationship, not to mention creating a space for calmness (see Chapter 7). Therefore, dogs need to be allowed in the house and should not spend most of their days alone in the backyard. If we offer our dog an open door to the outside, they will ultimately ignore it and stay inside with us. They want to be part of the family! Most dogs also prefer quality time with their humans over the biggest of backyards. Arguably, they have lost an important dog characteristic – the very one we appreciate dogs for – if they like being alone away from humans! I also think we miss out if we do not share living spaces with our dogs.

Research shows that humans who allow their dogs in the house are more attached to their dogs[24]. This is due to several factors, but I think that time together – the chance to have prolonged, passive exposure to one another – is what allows for that attachment. Plus, nothing is more relaxing than patting our dogs, for them and for us! So, while our dogs benefit from being in the house, so do we.

This also relates back to Arnold's bond-based teaching ideas[25] (Section 3.1.1). If we let dogs live in proximity with us, they will adjust their activities to ours. They will rest when we rest, be active when we are active and will know when we go out. They will even learn if they are coming with us somewhere, or if they have to stay at home. Dogs who know these things are much easier to live with and behave appropriately in different daily contexts. This, again, takes a lot of time spent together.

 In real life A common complaint from humans is that their dog scratches on the door and wants to come in when they are at home. The question is: *How do I train my dog to stay outside?* That is the wrong question. The question should be: *How can I teach my dog to be a good family member and behave appropriately inside, so that we can enjoy one another in the house?* Dogs should not be outside, alone, when we are at home; they should be inside with us. To make this work I recommend teaching them to be calm inside (see Chapter 7 and Section 9.7.3).

Ultimately, it takes time to really get to know someone. Yet, we often do not take the time to educate ourselves what it means to live in a multi-species family environment and how to train our dogs effectively. We assume that they like the same things we do; for example, being hugged, listening to loud music or having visitors over. We often do not realise that these situations might stress out our dogs. We also expect them to stay outside of the kitchen or off the lounge without explaining it to them. Living with another species is a two-way street. We need to learn how to adapt as well – we cannot expect our dogs to do all the work. We need to meet them in the middle and this is a learning process that takes a lot of time together. This means we might have to change our routine and get used to early rising, always having treats nearby and accepting that they might not like our music – and that we need to give ourselves and our dogs time and patience to learn about one another as individuals.

3.2.2 Realistic expectations

We need to have realistic views of our dogs, including how they develop and behave. No dog arrives perfectly trained – they all need work. Depending on the breed, the work we need to put in is different. Getting high-drive dogs in suburbia without much time to spare is a recipe for disaster. Some breeds might need less exercise, but they still need quality time with their humans. There is no such thing as a 'low maintenance dog'. They are all sentient beings with their own needs.

We also tend to forget that dogs are a 12-16 year commitment. We might miss out on the designer apartment because it is not dog-friendly or the promotion because we cannot take our dog to Paris. We don't consider that they will need two to three hours a day of our time and that we will, inevitably, lose something valuable in the process of them growing up (forget the cushions but think Persian rug, prescription glasses or grandma's jewellery). They cost a lot of money, require regular medical check-ups and, depending on the breed, this can be extremely expensive. For example, some of the short-muzzled (brachycephalic) breeds now need regular surgery to improve breathing. We also do not anticipate that they want to be with us, always! That includes going to the bathroom (just joking, you can train them not to come to the bathroom with you!).

3.2.3 Communication, trust and listening to our dogs

As any therapist will tell you, part of a good relationship is clear communication and its associated trust. We need to be clear about what we are saying to our dogs. Without clearly explaining what we want, our dogs probably feel like we would if we were living in a completely different culture without being taught what the 'correct' behaviour is. Imagine you are relaxing in bed and someone starts yelling at you in a strange language. They are clearly upset, throwing their arms around with an angry tone and a red face. You get out of bed, but don't know what you're supposed to do now to make them happy. They hit you and you're left confused about what the issue is, or your place in the household. You would certainly be left less trusting of this person. This is where this book comes in: you can learn how to communicate with your dog in a way that makes sense to them while also building up a two-way street of trust.

The flip side of expecting our dogs to learn human communication is that we need to learn dog communication. I like how Horowitz (Columbia University) puts it in her book[26]:

> 'The trouble, of course, with asking a dog if he is happy or depressed is not that the question makes no sense. It's that we are very poor at understanding his response. We're made terribly lazy by language.'

While they do not speak English (or German, or Swahili or Filipino) dogs communicate well – but only if we 'listen'. Or, more accurately, if we watch carefully. Dogs communicate mostly with body language. For example, dogs have the right and ability to say *no* and we need to accept and understand that answer when they do. Most are really nice about it and just walk away or turn their heads. However, if we miss those polite signs and force them into a hug, an outfit or an uncomfortable situation, they might growl or snap. Additionally, trust has been broken.

Ultimately, we try to train our dog so they participate voluntarily in their training; if we give them some control over what happens to them, they don't have to growl or snap. Having a good relationship with our dog and being able to understand what they are 'saying' will make training much easier. Body language is how we are able to recognise when our dog gets stressed or is uncomfortable, especially when dealing with an emotional teenage dog. We need to make an effort to understand their main way of communication – hackles, ears, tail, posture. This is our responsibility.

Darcy saying no loud and clear; he is completely disengaged with his human, who goes one way while he goes the other way. To be fair, he is also a clown and a typical teenager. He is not stressed, just distracted and joyfully doing his own thing – smiling at the photographer. Picture Le Hammer

Most of us will recognise when dogs are really upset. This is when they growl, snap, are very stiff, stare and their hackles are up. Still clear but a bit less obvious signs for some of us include them having their tail tucked under, crouching, ears back or when they lie down or paw. Early stress signs are often completely missed but recognising these is the first step towards de-escalating the situation.

The early stress signs have different names. Some trainers call them displacement behaviours, stress signs or calming signals. I like *displacement behaviours* because it describes what we see: a normal behaviour that is displayed out-of-context. The main ones are yawning, lip-licking, head-turning, scratching, shake-offs and intent sniffing. Humans, and other animals, do the same thing when feeling anxious – for example, when stressed, yawning or scratching are more common and occur more often out-of-context. Of course, dogs will yawn when they are tired, lick their lips if we hold a treat in front of their nose, turn their head if someone enters the room, scratch when they are itchy, sniff when there is an interesting smell, shake off when they are wet. However, if they yawn, lick their lips or turn their head away when we ask them to *sit* or start scratching or sniffing intently when another dog approaches, then this might be a sign of stress. We often see shake-offs after two dogs have been playing and it got a bit intense; they separate and shake-off the tension.

Next time our teenage dog has forgotten what *sit* or other well-practiced cues mean in a busy location; we should watch for displacement behaviours. Our dogs are probably stressed. When we see these stress signs it is better not to insist and accept that in this specific situation, they just cannot do it – even a simple *sit*! While stress is a normal part of life and cannot be avoided, too much stress is not conducive to learning – it may, in fact, inhibit learning (see Section 4.5). Additionally, stress can affect overall physical health and lifespan.

Chapter 3

 In real life I did a trick demonstration with Shellbe when she was about 15 months old – a real teenager. We were on stage (with a microphone) and there was a big audience. I asked her for a *sit* so I could have a chat with the presenter before the demo. She looked at me blankly. I could also see that she was a little stressed, as she licked her lips and yawned. We had trained, she was used to crowds, she had been on that stage before. But in that instant, she just could not do it. And I did not insist. Well, I admit it looks bad if the dog who should do a trick demo cannot *sit* on cue. Fortunately, I had already taught Shellbe what to do in situations where she felt overwhelmed. Our default behaviour if she gets stressed is that she puts her head on my shoulder and we both take a few deep breaths. I told the presenter that I needed to have a 'quick chat' to her before we could go on. That got us the laughs from the audience I had hoped for and gave her a bit of time for recovery. After a few seconds she was back on-track. I made sure not to ask for a *sit* again but went straight into the more difficult tricks. She performed like a star.

We need to respect these communicative signals our dogs are sending us. Our relationship has to be based on mutual trust. Our dogs have their own needs and feelings and these need to be considered in our daily interactions. They also have off-days, feel the heat or the cold or other stressors in their lives. The use of outdated and aversive training methods has no place in modern dog training. Our dogs need to be able to feel safe in our presence.

If our dog does not comply with our cue, then it is *our* responsibility to figure out why not. There might be too many distractions or stress, our dog might be having an off-day or they might be in pain. Jumping to the conclusion that our dog is disobedient or stubborn is not helpful. Often it is purely a case of incomplete training. In these cases, it is best to take a deep breath, take them out of the situation they don't cope with and go back to basics. Train in a less distracting environment, refresh our training and use better treats.

On the positive side, we also need to recognise when our dogs are communicating that they are happy and relaxed. In this state, their eyes are their normal size, they brows are smooth and they have a wrinkle-free forehead (although not the Shar-Peis!). They blink often and their gaze is soft. Their ears are floppy and their mouth can be open; their entire body is loose, soft and often wiggly. Most of us will recognise a happy dog, or at least we think so.

One common misconception is that a wagging tail means a happy dog. Not necessarily so! If their wagging tail is high up and moving fast in a back-and-forth motion while their body seems stiff, our dog is probably not happy but is, rather, on alert. If their tail is low and wagging slowly, they might be hesitant. However, if our dog is wagging their tail back and forth gently and the rest of their body is loose, their mouth is slightly open and they are panting gently, they are most likely happy. Fast wagging tails with other happy signals usually indicate that they are excited.

There are a lot of things that make our dogs happy and help to build trust. For example, most dogs love being touched – a gentle massage will be bliss for them. Different dogs do have different preferences for where and how they prefer to be touched and we need to figure out those individual preferences by learning how to understand what they are saying. We can detect our dog's preferences by touching different parts of their body and gauging their reactions. Dogs will indicate what they like or not by 'asking' us to do more, for example with a nose nudge, or less, by moving away. Horowitz also mentions that some dogs, especially young dogs, prefer full-body contact[27]. My young dog likes to lie next to me, his body touching mine from head to tail, while the older one prefers just a light touch on her back when curled up next to me. In my experience, dogs prefer repeated touches over constant pressure.

That is why we pat them rather than hug them, as most dogs do not really like being hugged. Learning what makes our dogs happy means we have a better idea of what would act as a positive reinforcer, as well as recognising their individuality (see Section 9.6). Through attentive communication, we are building a relationship of trust.'

3.2.4 Providing choice

An overlooked aspect of being happy and content is having choice and control over the outcome of our actions. Having no control over the outcome of our actions can be a major stressor for us and can even create anxiety. The same goes for our dogs (and other animals). They need some choice and we should try to give them more choices on a daily basis.

Choice is a fundamental condition for wellbeing; *choice is empowering*. Choice is also intrinsically rewarding and a primary reinforcer. This means – for example, in the context of husbandry behaviours such as nail trimming – that being able to stop the procedure if it becomes too much is, in itself, reinforcing for our dogs. This is similar to some clever dentists now giving their patients a stop button. How much of a relief is that?

The concept of choice is not new in dog training. However, the early approaches did not present any real choices because there was only one outcome that led to something positive. For example, one of the early mentions of choice came from Garrett, a dog trainer successful in Agility[28]. Her version of 'it's-your-choice training game' is a classic example of only one positive outcome. The concept of the game is simple: teach your dog that in order to get what they want, first they must do what you want. Or, as Garrett says on her website[29]:

> 'Find something of great value to your dog (a few pieces of cheese, his favourite treat) and create an environment that will eventually encourage him to make the right choice (which is what you want) before you give him his reward (which is what he wants).'

In this case, we are just manipulating our dog into doing what we want them to do. Another example is that we let the dog decide if they want to participate in a training session and they are free to leave. While this choice is a basic prerequisite in positive reinforcement training, if nothing interesting is happening outside the training session, leaving is not a real choice. These 'choices' are like going into an ice cream shop and the only flavour available is vanilla. There is nothing wrong with vanilla, but this is not a real choice.

Giving real choice means there are several rewarding options available. This can mean giving our dogs several options for resting places, letting them choose which way to go on a walk or asking them what they would like for dinner. Providing real alternatives means that we are leaving reinforcers such as a food-dispensing toy in the training area and if the dog decides not to participate in the training, they have a real, fun, alternative choice of something to do and can access the toy. This does not mean we never remove distraction to set them up for success (see Section 9.2). There is a difference between giving choice and having too many distractions to make training possible; I recommend having at least one good alternative choice for them in case they don't want to participate. This also provides feedback for us. If they choose the alternative, our training might not be as good as we thought and we might have to improve our training techniques. Astonishingly, if the teaching is done well, most dogs will still participate in the training, probably because they love the social interaction (this also relates to the contra-freeloading concept, described in Section 8.2.1). Ultimately, when dogs realise that they have a choice and that they can stop something scary by simply walking away, they learn to trust us and they will become more inclined to participate voluntarily.

A caveat to the idea of providing choice is that while we should try to give our dogs enticing options, it is not always possible for them to get what they want, and sometimes there is just one choice. It is like work for us humans. We either go to work and get paid or we don't. For our dogs, in some training situations, this means *you do what I am asking and get the reinforcer* or *you don't and there is no payment*. Even then, though, our dogs are exerting some level of choice – they can choose no ice cream over vanilla if they want.

Modern training now talks about providing real alternatives by teaching 'start-button behaviours' and 'mand behaviours'. *Start-button behaviours* are behaviours that indicate to us that our dog is ready to start training or a husbandry procedure. The *head-rest* described in Section 9.8.6 is an example; if our dog puts their chin on our hand, they are saying it is *ok* to proceed, but if they leave that position, they are saying *no* and we need to stop. Patel's bucket game[30] is another example: as long as our dog looks at the bucket they are consenting, if they look away, this means *no*.

Mand behaviours are a request; our dog is communicating a need in a specific situation. Dogs might sit in front of the door because they need to go out, drop the ball in front of us for a play, nudge us for a pat or give us those pleading eyes when they would like a bite of our sandwich. These are all requests for something from us.

 In real life An example of a dog making a request is when my dog Chillax pushes his water bowl – loudly – around the deck when it is empty. Chillax only does it when the bowl is empty, he never pushes it around when it is full. There are two options for dealing with this: yell at him and tell him to stop because it is noisy or pay attention and see this as him clearly communicating a need. My husband and I now fill up his water bowl if he starts pushing it around (we obviously also make sure it is full most of the time). I have no problem with this behaviour, but it might not be suitable if you live in an apartment. In that case, gently nudging the empty water bowl might be more suitable. Chillax will also bring his leash when he would like to go for a quick stroll in the late afternoon. In most cases I will take him for a quick walk, since he asked so nicely.

I can already hear you say *'but then I have to do whatever my dogs wants and needs'*. Well… yes and no. If our dog communicates a real need like water then yes, we should attend to this immediately. If they want to go out then we might teach them *'soon'*, meaning *'be patient until I have finished what I am doing'* (see Section 9.8.1) or we can redirect them to an appropriate alternative like a puzzle. Either way, 'mand behaviours' will make sure their needs are met and they have choice and control. It can also reduce problem behaviours because our dogs communicate their needs and then have faith that we will pay attention to what they are asking for. I recommend listening and, whenever possible, attending to their needs.

3.3 Summary

Considering dogs as friends or family with their own complex needs and as sentient beings is the best way to approach our relationship with our teenage dogs. However, the relationship is not a straight-forward matter of unconditional love. We have to work at creating and maintaining the relationship, including a shift in mindset away from the historical dominance- based approach to human-dog relationships. This will change the language we use. We will use *cues* instead of *commands* and call ourselves *humans* or *guardians* instead of *owners*.

To form a meaningful relationship with our dogs we need to spend quality time with them (inside) and have realistic expectations. We need to learn to clearly communicate so we can foster trust and treat them with respect. This will help our dogs and us to form a secure attachment. Giving our teenage dogs more choice in a world that is difficult to navigate will make for more satisfying relationships. Real choices, 'start button' and 'mand behaviours' might seem a bit farfetched for some, however, I do believe this will become mainstream soon, as people shift their mentality (and language) towards a friend-based relationship with their dogs, rather than a dominance-based one.

Chapter 4
Anthropomorphism and emotions – Do dogs really have feelings?

There is still a stigma attached to talking about animal emotions. Humans are humans and supposedly have all these emotions that other animals do not. To acknowledge that dogs experience joy, sadness or grief in a similar way as humans do can be confronting and even scary because we would have to change the way we treat them. And not only them, but all animals. If we do not make these changes, future generations will undoubtedly ask: '*how in the world could you do what you did knowing what you knew about the cognitive and emotional lives of other animals?*'[31].

4.1 The scientific sin of anthropomorphism and talking about animal minds

The traditional argument about animal minds used to go along the lines of: because you cannot objectively see a thought or a feeling, it is considered unscientific to presume animals have them; the mind is an unknowable, unmeasurable 'black box'. Anthropomorphism – the attribution of human traits, emotions, goals, and thoughts to nonhumans – is considered to be a scientific 'sin' since it lacks objectivity (by making assumptions about an animal's mind). Far more scientifically conservative is to focus on behaviours. Even the Diploma in Canine Behaviour Science and Technology I graduated from was only focusing on observable behaviours and how we can change these (unwanted) behaviours using mainly applied behaviour analysis, without reference to dog minds. *Behaviour analysis* is a technique that uses learning principles to create a behaviour change and focuses solely on observable behaviours. Talking about how dogs *feel* about certain stimuli or situations was consider unhelpful or unscientific, whereas talking about how they *react* to stimuli or situations was measurable, provable and knowable.

Indi having fun on the beach. I don't think we need research, statistics or publications to see that Indi is enjoying himself. There is nothing wrong in attributing feelings to our dogs because they are clearly visible and it helps in understanding them better. Picture Grazia Pecoraro.

While behaviour analysis *is* an important part of behaviour modification, I think we need to take emotions into account when living and interacting with our dogs, and probably even more so with our teenage dogs. Imagine, after all, that you were tasked with living with and loving a moody, emotional teenage human but you could only 'read' their behaviour, not their mind (words or thoughts). Our view of that person would probably be pretty impoverished – and yet this is considered the scientific approach to animal minds!

4.2 Primary emotions

In terms of what scientific studies have been able to uncover about dog minds through indirect evidence, it is generally agreed that basic/primary emotional states (reactions to events/situations) such as anger, happiness and fear are present; they are evolutionarily adaptive and are associated with neural structures within the limbic system and specific neurotransmitter balance in the brain[32]. Panksepp, for one, believes that all mammals experience joy (which he calls the PLAY system), sadness and grief (PANIC/LOSS system), anger (RAGE system), anxiety and fear (FEAR system), lust (MATING system), enthusiasm and desire (SEEKING system) and tenderness and love (CARE system)[33]. The brain of our dog has all the basic structures and connections supporting basic emotional functions.

Another way at looking at it is from an affective neuroscience point of view, with a consideration of how dog emotions tie into relationships with their humans. There is evidence that neural reward systems are activated when dogs smell their humans, they release oxytocin when they lock eyes with their humans and cortisol levels reduce in stressful situations after human interaction[34]. Berns and colleagues did research on how the dog's part of the brain linked to positive associations (the caudate nucleus) responds to the scent of familiar humans compared to their own scent, the scent of a strange human, a familiar dog and an unfamiliar dog[35]. They found that the dogs discriminated the scent of the familiar human and that they had a positive emotional association with it.

So, we know that dogs attend to social cues and respond to facial expressions and scents of humans. They also behave differently according to the emotional situation and have emotionally-driven expectations. This is a fancy way of saying that dogs have emotions – and it has been measured. This is probably unsurprising to anyone who has a dog (especially a teenage one!).

However, it should be noted that in relation to Berns findings, the fact that reward centres in the dogs' brains are activated when they smell their human does not necessarily mean that they *love* those humans. The result could indicate an emotional attachment *or* it could be explained through conditioning (e.g. the humans repeatedly paired with food). The saying *the way to a man's heart is through his stomach* probably applies to dogs and all other animals, too.

As another example of why we need to think carefully about our assumptions of dog behaviour and emotions, consider the scenario of coming home to find rubbish scattered across the kitchen floor and a guilty-looking dog avoiding eye contact. A study by Horowitz suggests that there might be better explanation for the 'guilty look' than guilt itself: it is a learnt or instinctive response to the appearance of an angry or scolding human[36]. In her experiment, and on the uncountable videos we see on social media, the reaction of the dogs are most likely appeasement behaviours (such as avoiding eye contact, lying down and rolling to the side or onto the back, dropping their tail, wagging low and quickly, holding their ears back or head down, moving away, raising a paw, licking) in response to the threatening body language of the humans, not in response to their own feelings of guilt. In Horowitz's experiment the scolding behaviour of the humans increased the appeasement behaviours, whether or not the dogs had done something wrong (the human participants were lied to about their dog breaking a rule). 'The results indicate that the so-called guilty look is a response to owner scolding; it is not expressed more often when actually guilty'[37]. However, Horowitz also points out that her research does not prove that dogs do not experience guilt but, rather, that what we think of as 'guilty' behaviours may be attributed to something else.

These are prime examples of maintaining a scientifically objective stance about animal minds (albeit interpersonally unrewarding). Additionally, while we don't know if dogs love us or feel guilt the same way we love them or others, we need to be aware that *our* [human] love and feelings of guilt are *also* the result of evolution and conditioning – there is nothing demeaning in talking about emotions in this way, for humans or dogs.

4.3 Secondary emotions

The presence of secondary emotions (emotional reactions to other emotions; feeling about feeling) such as pride or Schadenfreude are not well researched but are probably not in our dogs' repertoire. However, Kujala[38] (University of Helsinki) does interesting research on a sense of fairness, empathy and jealousy, which are more complex social emotions that depend on interactions with others. These studies highlight several similarities between dogs and humans. It seems that dogs do have a sense of fairness (as do other animals such as primates). In an experiment done by Brucks and colleagues[39] (University of Vienna), dogs were rewarded either equally or unequally for giving their paw. The dog not rewarded for giving their paw refused to keep giving their paw when they knew another dog *was* rewarded for the same behaviour. They also interacted less with the experimenter or the other dog in a social setting after the experiment; it was as if they held a grudge about the inequity. People who feel they have been treated unfairly can probably relate.

One article mentions that the co-evolution and domestication of dogs and their associated social-communicative skills might have created their capacity for jealousy and even cross-species jealousy[40]. This is another indicator of how we have shaped dogs' behaviour (and minds) through the process of co-domestication. What about empathy? Again, studies 'show that at least emotional contagion is possible in dogs'[41] and post-conflict affiliation may indicate empathic concern. To take this one step further Kujala mentions that it is possible that dogs have unique emotional states that humans don't have, linked to their olfactory world. Ultimately, more research is needed in order to assess the extent of complex, secondary emotions in dogs.

4.4 Reconsidering anthropomorphism and animal minds

As you can see, we have now started to seriously consider the inner lives of animals despite the 'sin' of anthropomorphism. Authors such as Burghardt (University of Tennessee) make the case for *critical anthropomorphism*, meaning that we use our own human intuition and understanding as a starting point to understand animal cognition and then marry that with theory, evidence, science and critical analysis[42]. We are, after all, fellow animals, so it is probably more scientific to assume dogs (and other animals) are like us than to assume they are unfeeling and machine-like (the traditional approach).

Kujala[43] points out that it is not possible to scientifically and objectively demonstrate that dogs feel emotions, but that the same is true for all other species, including humans. Despite the lack of evidence for emotions in humans, we can all understand that that doesn't mean they aren't happening. Similarly, despite science's reluctance to accept animal minds, those of us who love animals understand that that doesn't mean they aren't there.

Martin (Kennesaw State University) makes an interesting point by arguing 'that ascribing an emotion is primarily a description of a behavioral pattern'[44]. If, for example, we say 'You seem afraid', it is a well-accepted shortcut for describing that we saw a person flinch, move away, scan the environment or whatever else that gives us the impression that the person thinks something bad might happen. Some of these behaviours are public (eye movement when scanning the environment) or private (the thoughts), voluntary (moving away) and involuntary (flinch). This suggests that it is not unreasonable to use behaviour as an indicator of internal thought processes, even if we cannot 'prove' it scientifically. For example, if we see our sleeping dog wake up suddenly and look around (both measurable) when something heavy is dropped, it is reasonable to assume that they were startled (not directly measurable). I am sure all of us living with dogs are pretty accurate at realising when our dogs are scared and the behaviours they show in these instances – there's no need to access the 'black box' directly when the behaviours themselves indicate internal processes. The difference to objective scientific approaches is that we need not stop our interpretation at the behavioural level – we consider their minds and emotions as well. Because the behaviours dogs express are very similar to the ones humans show when we are afraid, we can intuitively understand [at least] some of our dogs' thoughts and feelings.

While we are currently not able to say with certainty *how* dogs (and humans or other animals) feel, we can say with certainty that *they have feelings*. Rushing to an unsupported conclusion that animals are *just like us* is bad and is the bias that behaviourists were trying to avoid in their science. But, wilfully ignoring evidence of animal behaviours that look suspiciously like human emotions is unscientific and biased, too[45]. Anthropomorphism is appropriate if applied in an appropriate way. Safina's book *Beyond Words – What Animals Think and Feel*[46] is a great starting point to discover how other species perceive the world and how they feel. So are the books *The Emotional Lives of Animals: A Leading Scientist Explores Animal Joy, Sorrow, and Empathy – And Why They Matter* by Bekoff[47] and *Are We Smart Enough to Know How Smart Animals Are?* by de Waal[48].

4.5 Stress and learning

A key point to keep in mind is that our dog can become stressed and we need to be attentive to the signs of stress (see Section 3.2.3) to ensure we are not doing things that might increase this undesirable emotion. This includes being careful about how we train and being aware that our training might be counterproductive if we try to just 'push through' our dog being stressed. The effects of stress on learning have been well-recognised in animals[49] and depend on the type, duration and level of the stress being experienced. For example, sustained stress can impair explicit cognition that stems from the hippocampus, due to a decrease in neural synaptic plasticity[50]. Without these synaptic links, the brain resorts to amygdala-dependent (or, more emotionally- and fear/anxiety-dependent) responses – an obvious problem for teenage dogs who already rely more on emotions than cognition for problem-solving. Conversely, it is possible for feelings of fear to be linked to particular stressful environments, situations, people or dogs as a sort of implicit memory enhancement through classical conditioning (also called 'flashbulb memories' or 'one event learning'; see Section 9.1.2). These are often the stress-related memories that we must actively decrease given how strongly they can tint our dog's feelings about particular stimuli.

From a different perspective, stimulation and enrichment that require problem-solving (see Section 8.2.1) can be considered a form of mild and temporary stress. Mild and temporary stress provides an appropriate level of challenge, which then enhances synaptic plasticity and cognition[51]. In other words, learning is enhanced through the opportunity to be stimulated and enriched. Thus, it is critical that we ensure our dog is not overly stressed during training sessions due to the negative effects stress can have on learning (or the unhelpful memory-enhanced effects of fear), but we also need to provide an appropriate degree of mild challenge (or a job) that actually enhanced the brain's engagement with learning (see Section 8.2.1).

4.6 Training animal minds *and* bodies

What does an acknowledgment of dog minds and stress mean, in terms of training? It essentially means we need to ask *why* are our dogs doing things, rather than *what* they are doing. When dealing with unwanted behaviours we need to figure out two things: firstly, what is the function of the unwanted behaviour (what does it accomplish for our dog?); and secondly, what do we want them to do instead (an acceptable behaviour for us and our dogs)?

Let's assume our dog jumps up on people to greet them (teenage dogs are often the main culprits in this scenario because they are enthusiastic about wanting to meet visitors). The function of this behaviour is getting access to the person; our dog wants to meet them. We need to acknowledge that request and provide a more acceptable option that meets their need. For example, a good alternative is *sit-for-greeting*. This is incompatible with jumping up because our dog cannot jump and *sit* at the same time. However, in order to ensure that this is still rewarding for our dog, the visitors need to be willing to give our dog attention when they *sit* by going down to their level, patting them and maybe giving them a treat. If our dog can meet the person when they *sit* then we have fulfilled their needs, too – they gain access. We (and our visitors!) need to adapt to our dog's behaviour so that they can, in turn, adapt to our expectations. Dog training is a two-way street.

Another common problem (for some people) is our dog wanting to be on the couch with us. My dogs are allowed on the couch but let's assume they are not in your house. The function of this behaviour is having a comfortable and warm place to sleep near us. An alternative that still caters for this need is a comfortable dog bed in the loungeroom near the couch. In this case, the alternative behaviour is *go-to-mat* (see Section 9.8.1 for how to teach this). For every unwanted behaviour there is one that has the same function and is acceptable for us humans. I admit, sometimes it takes a bit of time to figure it out. But, given we are the ones with the bigger brains and more planning abilities (see Section 2.2.1), we should be able to do it. For example, digging can be addressed by giving them a specific area where they can dig or a sand pit. Inappropriate biting and chewing can be helped with chew toys and treasure hunts for treats in the garden. Dogs hump for different reasons; for example, because they are excited or stressed or because it feels good, in play or to self-sooth. Humping can be redirected to a game of fetch or tug, which can decrease excitement and release stress. By addressing what our dog wants in these situations, we are better prepared for how to train an alternative, acceptable behaviour.

Training tip Once we have figured out what we would like our dog to do, an important part of the process is to teach the 'good' behaviour outside of the problematic context. Going back to the jumping-up-on-visitors example: we teach a *sit-stay* and practice in different environments and reward generously. We then make sure our dog understands the *sit-stay* cue in many different situations. We aim for a long history of reinforcement and rehearsal for sitting. Once we are sure our dog understands *sit-stay* in all (or at least most) contexts, then – and only then – do we go back to the situation where the dog is likely to jump and we get ready for it! If our dog approaches the visitor at the door, we ask for a *sit* before they jump and then we reinforce the sitting. If our dog jumps up, we take a deep breath (yes, we made a mistake) wait for a *sit* and reinforce. We do not cue the *sit*; the dog needs to find out what gets them the treat (see Section 9.5 for more information on why we do not ask for a *sit*). Do not yell or push the dog down – this just might be the game they were waiting for! Pushing down and yelling, if done hard and they perceive it as aversive, is positive punishment (which I don't recommend; see Chapter 5). If we manage carefully, we should get a reliable *sit-stay* very quickly. It is important to set them up for success. If the *sit-stay* is not reliable, we should not allow the dog near the door when their favourite friend arrives. This is where management comes in (see Section 9.4). Once they sit, our visitors should give them the attention they want so we have addressed their need, too.

4.7 Summary

It is relatively 'taboo' to talk about animal minds within scientific approaches to animal behaviour, despite the growing research into primary and secondary emotions. However, some behaviourists are starting to reconsider this 'sin', using critical anthropomorphism. Overall, while we do not know what dogs feel exactly, most of us who live with dogs will probably agree with Jane Goodall: 'You cannot share your life with a dog [...] and not know perfectly well that animals have personalities and minds and feelings'[52]. Luckily, this has now started to filter down in how dogs are treated in our laws. For example, in September 2019, the Australian Capital Territory introduced new laws which consider pets as sentient beings. I am confident that similar laws will follow the more we learn about animal cognition, emotions and social responses.

While waiting for such welfare laws to be enacted in our local area and science to catch up to what most of us know already, we should be attentive to what it means to treat the root of our dog's problematic behaviour – which means acknowledging their minds, emotions, needs, stress, desires and preferences. We should aim to fulfil our dog's needs, too, by paying attention to what they want and what the function is of a specific behaviour and then find and teach an alternative, more-acceptable behaviour for that need – something that is acceptable for us and our dog.

Chapter 5
Best practice? – Positive reinforcement training methods

We all agree that we need to train – or should we say *teach* – our dogs to co-exist in human worlds. However, the methods we are using are still up for discussion, which is surprising, given that there is a lot of information and solid scientific research that positive reinforcement is more effective, and has fewer side effects, than other methods. This has been proven by scientific studies and research[53] and is argued by animal behaviourists[54]. Positive reinforcement training methods are associated with higher levels of obedience and fewer problematic behaviours. Dogs trained with positive methods are less attention-seeking, aggressive or fearful and will have more success in future training[55]. Perhaps one of the main advantages of positive reinforcement training is that it does not cause aggression, which can emerge from more aversive methods.

Almost all reputable professional organisations – including (in Australia) Pet Professional Guild Australia[56], Delta Institute[57], Australian Veterinary Association[58] and The Association of Pet Dog Trainers Australia[59] – will recommend positive reinforcement as their preferred options. The only organisation in Australia that still maintains that punishment is necessary is the National Dog Trainers Federation[60], but even they have toned it down compared to only a few years ago (they now describe their approach as 'balanced' which sounds good but is a euphemism for using punishment).

I tend to compare dog training to educating children. While dogs are not humans, all beings learn the same way – by the consequences a behaviour has, good or bad. In the 'good old days' a smack to a kid here and there was considered acceptable. But this has changed; here in Australia corporal punishment in schools became illegal in the 1990s. Considering that we decided that punishment wasn't the way to go with children over 30 years ago, I feel it is probably not the way to go with dogs, either. This sentiment is shared by those who let go of concepts of dominance and hierarchies by accepting the newer, less relationship-damaging methods of teaching and training. Most behaviour problems we see with unruly teenage dogs are not caused by dominance issues but by a lack of training and socialisation, or anxiety and the lack of control over their environment. It is our job to guide our dogs towards socially-acceptable behaviour (as we do with children and teenagers) rather than to punish them for breaking a rule they were never informed of. They don't need an alpha – they need a friend (see Chapter 3).

5.1 What is positive reinforcement and how does it compare against other training methods?

There is a lot of talk about the four quadrants in dog training, as shown in the table. So-called 'balanced' dog trainers insist that using all four quadrants is necessary in training (this is the National Dog Trainers Federation stance). However, as mentioned earlier, positive reinforcement trainers will only use one or maybe two of the quadrants and science confirms that this works best.

Overall, the four quadrants are a helpful but limited construct and only covers what we call *operant conditioning* (for information on *respondent conditioning* see Section 9.1.2). Operant conditioning deals with teaching behaviours such as *sit, lie-down*, etc. It is a

> 'learning process in which the likelihood of a specific behavior increases or decreases in response to reinforcement or punishment that occurs when the behavior is exhibited, so that the subject comes to associate the behavior with the pleasure from the reinforcement or the displeasure from the punishment.'[61]

In other words, we are using reinforcement to strengthen a behaviour or to get more of this specific behaviour in the operant training context. *Positive reinforcement* means we are adding something to get more of a behaviour; for example, we are adding a treat, praise or play when our dog *sits*. We often call the treat a *reward* but I prefer calling it a *reinforcer*, because this describes more accurately what it is: adding something that increases a behaviour. *Negative reinforcement* means we are taking something unpleasant away to increase a behaviour; for example, we stop yelling at our dog when they *sit* after jumping up on us, or we use a collar that shocks our dog until they come back or we release the check chain when our dog is in the correct healing position.

	Positive	Negative
Reinforcement	Add something to increase a behaviour	Take something unpleasant away to increase behaviour (something bad or unpleasant has to happen beforehand)
Punishment	Add something to decrease a behaviour	Remove something the dog likes to decrease the behaviour

Four quadrants in dog training

We are using punishment to reduce a behaviour. If we use *positive punishment*, we add something unpleasant. For example, we hit our dog when they do the wrong thing or we yell or jerk on the leash when they aren't walking in the correct position. With *negative punishment* we take something away to reduce a behaviour. For example, we turn our back on our dog when they jump and therefore stop giving them the attention they are wanting. Note that negative or positive does not mean bad or good. It just means we either take something away (negative) or add something (positive) to get more (reinforcement) or less (punishment) of a behaviour.

Some examples of what these four forms of training look like: We could give our dog a treat when they sit (positive reinforcement) or we could push our dog's rear down and release pressure when they sit (negative reinforcement). We can yell at our dog when they jump up (positive punishment) or we can ignore our dog when they jump up (negative punishment). I know it sounds confusing but if we take a bit of time to understand the concept it makes sense and is a useful framework. All methods described in the four quadrants will eventually teach the dog what we want, but there are undesirable side effects of certain methods.

While positive punishment works to suppress behaviour (that is what it is supposed to do), it also has severe fallouts[62]. Dogs might try to avoid us or revert to aggression. They might become afraid or aggressive towards others who were in the vicinity when we hurt them, or they might shut down or get depressed. Our relationship with them is, essentially, threatened.

On top of this, the brains of our teenage dogs are not processing information correctly even without the added stress of aversive training methods. Imagine how their emotionally-reactive brains will struggle with making correct decisions when we add punishment into the mix! This can lead to severe aggression or a complete shutdown in any dog, but even more so for teenage dogs. They are now not only dealing with a brain that has difficulties processing information correctly but also with stress and fear. The stress these methods create inhibits learning (see Section 4.5). Punitive methods often lead to dogs who look calm but if we watch their body language carefully, they are stressed and what we see is called *learnt helplessness*[63]. Learnt helplessness is a state of feeling powerlessness. In the case of dogs, it is often caused by aversive stimuli beyond their control and which they cannot escape.

My main concern with the use of aversive methods is the welfare of our dogs and our relationships with them. Punishment affects the bond between us and our dogs and it can make our dogs scared and less trusting of us, especially if our own aggressive behaviour is positively reinforced. It might make our dog reluctant to try new things and they might not offer new behaviours. Additionally, our dogs [understandably] do not want to spend time with us if we hurt them, which means both we and they lose out on a trusting relationship.

A literature review by Ziv[64] (Wingate Institute) concluded:

> 'using aversive training methods (e.g., positive punishment and negative reinforcement) can jeopardize both the physical and mental health of dogs. In addition, while positive punishment can be effective, there is no evidence that it is more effective than positive reinforcement-based training. In fact, there is some evidence that the opposite is true. [...] In conclusion, those working with or handling dogs should rely on positive reinforcement methods, and avoid using positive punishment and negative reinforcement as much as possible.'

Positive reinforcement training only uses positive reinforcement and very limited negative punishment because these techniques have less side effects, are more pleasant and better for the relationship. Positive reinforcement trainers do not use positive punishment or negative reinforcement. We consider these methods inhumane, unethical and unnecessary because science has proven that positive reinforcement training simply works best.

Using punishment will only suppress behaviour without teaching a different more appropriate behaviour to fill the void. It also does not tackle the underlying cause of the problem, which can be addressed by focusing on positive reinforcement (see Section 4.6). Although some positive trainers support the use of negative punishment (e.g. turning away or taking attention away from our dog when they do something undesirable), many have moved on from ignoring our dog's 'bad' behaviour (see Section 8.2.3) by trying to manage the environment (see Section 9.4) and using interrupt – redirect – reinforce (see Section 9.3).

5.2 What does positive reinforcement look like?

As mentioned earlier, the aim of aversive methods is mostly to just suppress behaviour, for example the lunging and barking of a teenage dog at an unfamiliar person or object. In contrast, positive reinforcement trainers will figure out the cause of the behaviour – or what is going on in the 'black box' of our dog's mind (see Section 4.6). Often dogs are scared when they show these behaviours, which means we need to address the underlying fear to solve the problem. In order to address these fears, we use a process called *desensitising* and *counter-conditioning* to change our dog's perception of the stimulus. For example, if our teenage dog finds children on a skateboard scary, we are trying to change their negative emotional association to a positive one. Desensitising and counter-conditioning is using a second form of conditioning called *respondent conditioning* which changes how a dog feels about a certain stimulus (see Section 9.1.2 for how the process works exactly).

During this process it is important that we watch and learn to read our teenage dog. Dogs 'talk' to us all the time – but only when we watch. Dogs communicate with body language and the more fluent we are in reading what they say the better we understand them (see Section 3.2.3

on displacement behaviours and how to keep an open line of communication with our teenage dog). The better we understand their underlying thoughts and feelings, the better we can teach them appropriate alternative ways of behaving themselves. We also need to be careful about not trying to train them when they are stressed and overwhelmed (see Section 4.5).

When teaching our dogs what we would like them to do, we are breaking behaviours down into small achievable steps and are reinforcing the correct response. We are using three main ways of teaching: *luring*, *capturing* and *shaping*.

Luring

The first way of teaching is *luring*. A lure is a piece of food that guides our dog into the correct position. When the dog is in the position, we *mark* and *reinforce*. *Mark* means we communicate to our dog via a click (if we use a clicker) or a short word like '*yes*' indicating to them that they have done the right thing and a *reinforcer* will be delivered shortly (see Section 9.1.1 for a step-by-step guide and a more extensive explanation of marking and reinforcing).

Capturing

When *capturing* good behaviour (a second way of teaching) we reinforce appropriate behaviours our dog is already doing. If we see our dog do something we like (e.g. calmly lying on their bed), we will let them know by giving them something they want (food, toy or pat). We look out for an appropriate behaviour and reinforce it.

Shaping

A third way of teaching through positive reinforcement training is called *shaping*. When shaping a behaviour, we are working with approximations, where we reinforce behaviours that gradually become more refined and look more-and-more like the behaviour we are aiming for (see Section 9.1.1). Shaping can be great fun and lead to amazing results but it takes a bit of practice for both humans and dogs.

5.3 Positive reinforcement training for humans and unlearning old ways

In dog training we are teaching teams that consist of both humans and dogs. When teaching humans, we have long-since made the switch to positive reinforcement; no one considers positive punishment appropriate anymore and there are laws that prevent, for example teachers, using corporal punishment with students. I also don't think we would have a lot of willing human students in our classes if we used an aversive approach with them. However, when training dogs, often the humans have to first unlearn and let go of old ways; including ideas like that we need to dominate dogs, that we always need to control them and be the 'alpha' and that punishment is an effective way of communicating preferences (see Section 3.1.2). Unfortunately, these outdated ideas from the past are still in our heads and sometimes get the better of us.

For example, an undesirable side effect of using punishment that is not often discussed is that it can also be reinforcing for the human punisher and can then escalate and become a habit. This can occur because if a person is frustrated with their dog's behaviour and they hit or yell at the dog, they may feel better for the moment in which the behaviour stopped. This will cause the person to use it more often and possibly harder the next time. I feel this is what is happening with professional trainers who advocate the use of aversive methods; they are getting a 'kick' out of abusing dogs. How else can it be explained that these trainers purposefully set the dogs up to fail so they can use positive punishment? They ask the dog for a behaviour that has not been trained properly and then jerk, shock or yell when the dog gets it wrong.

Changing our way of thinking will need reflection and then time to practice the new ways. Once we understand that we all learn the same way and that positive reinforcement works for both humans and dogs, we then have a meaningful way of teaching our dogs through positive reinforcement methods.

If our dogs do not do what we are asking for, they are not dominant, stubborn or stupid. There are two main reasons for 'non-compliance' – both of which require us humans to reconsider our interactions with our dogs:

1) **They do not understand what we are asking them to do.** This means our training is incomplete and we must explain to them what we want better. We must go back to basics and help them understand the cues. Chances are, us humans did not explain what we wanted appropriately and although our dogs may want to do what we ask, they just don't understand what we are asking.

2) They understand what we want, but **there is not enough in it for them**. They have decided it isn't worth the effort; our reinforcer is not reinforcing enough. Remember, they need choice and this is a choice they get to make. It may be worth more to smell an interesting bush than to receive praise for returning to their human. We can 'fix' this by using better- and higher-value reinforcers or by training in less distractive environments (so that we become relatively more interesting to our dog). However, it is important to choose our battles wisely and sometimes we can and should accept our dog making a different choice.

5.4 Summary

Positive reinforcement methods are by far the best way to train dogs and are overall associated with better outcomes, less stress and a better relationship between us and our dogs. Aversive methods, which are based on outdated constructs of the social behaviour of dogs (such as dominance and the need for a pack leader), aim to suppress behaviour and are associated with severe side effects ranging from dogs shutting down emotionally to aggression. When using positive methods, we focus on changing perceptions and emotions by using *desensitising* and *counter-conditioning* and teaching our dogs by breaking things down into manageable steps. We reinforce the correct response with something they like, ensuring at the same time that the dogs feel safely bonded to us. We can use luring, capturing or shaping. Humans often need to first let go of the old ways of thinking and realise that all beings learn the same way and the use of force is counter-productive.

Chapter 6
Socialisation is a lifelong process

Socialisation is one of the 'buzz' words in dog training and everyone defines it differently. Socialisation at a basic level is *respondent (classical) conditioning* which means creating an association with a neutral or potentially scary stimulus (see Section 9.1.2). In the case of dog socialisation, we want to create a positive association with others (humans, dogs, other animals) and the environment (cars, trucks, bikes, surfaces, noises, different substrates, etc.) so our dog feels safe. Socialisation should cover any environment our dog needs to function in – and have a positive association with – like coffee shops, busy roads, shopping strips, beaches, tracks, groomers, vets, boarding facilities, etc.

It is common sense nowadays to socialise puppies, but there is a misconception that socialisation is *only* essential for puppies. Socialisation is not something we do for a couple months when we have time; socialisation is a lifelong process for both us and our dog. For example, we wouldn't expect our child to be an expert at navigating social situations just because they went to birthday parties when they were five years old. However, a lot of people assume that doing a puppy preschool and taking the puppy to a lot of places at a young age will be enough.

It is true that we should socialise our puppies carefully and extensively; four to 16-week old puppies are certainly in an important window of opportunity, which is when we get the most 'bang for our buck' in terms of socialisation. One or two positive associations – for example with a child, other animals, noises, different surfaces, older people, people with different ethnic backgrounds, cars, trucks, sirens – will make a lasting positive impression on our puppy. A properly-socialised puppy is more likely to perceive the world as a safe and fun place and ongoing socialisation as a teenage dog will be easier. An under-socialised puppy could be fearful of new things and might end up being cautious or even anxious and this might become more pronounced when they are teenagers.

Therefore, although socialisation begins during puppyhood, it is required at all life-stages. To make socialisation effective it needs to be an ongoing process, which means we need to expose our teenage dog to new experiences on a continual basis and in a positive way. Raising a well-adjusted dog is a lifelong commitment and socialisation during the teenage phase is as crucial as it is during puppyhood. If we do not keep up socialisation with our teenage dogs their ability to do well in new environments declines quickly. Even mature dogs benefit from social outings.

However, it is also important to keep in mind that dogs are a bit like us as they get older: they really do not want to interact with random dogs they meet (see Section 2.2.5). It is unrealistic to assume dogs will play indiscriminately with other dogs once they have reached social maturity, or that they will get along with every single dog they meet. Teenage dogs often still love to play and interact with 'new' friends but might start to prefer playing with their known friends and play dates with known dogs might work better than random meetings. Adult and elderly dogs require a different sort of socialisation; they do better with meeting their friends one-on-one or small groups of known dogs. There are also mature and older dogs who just do not want to meet new dogs and are more than happy to spend time with their humans, going on walks or for a swim, doing some training, learning a new trick or hanging out at the coffee shop.

There is discussion amongst trainers that creating a positive association with other dogs and humans could be counter-productive for our puppy and teenage dog. The argument is that if we create a positive association, our dog will find other people and dogs too interesting and will ignore us. This is the wrong discussion, not only because it is paramount to socialise our dogs well so they perceive the world (in general) and others (humans and dogs) as safe to approach and interact, but also because it denies them choice and the opportunity to have some control over the outcome of their actions (see Section 3.2.4). We need to establish their self-confidence outside of our relationship and their place within the home. Once we have created a positive association, we then teach our dog with operant conditioning that it is not necessary to interact with every single person or dog. This is much easier to do if the underlying association is a positive one; trying to train a dog who is scared is much more difficult (see Section 4.5). While we can never socialise our dog to everything (life is not a checklist, after all, and dogs will encounter unknown things), the more positive experiences they have, the better they can deal with new things. This starts with early socialisation, exposure and training.

6.1 Dogs in the human world

Fifty years ago, not too many people talked about dog socialisation. This is not because dogs did not need it, but because, for the most part, they 'self-socialised'. Dogs were less legally-regulated and physically-restricted than today. They wandered and roamed the neighbourhood, accompanied children to school, hung out with other dogs, sometimes got into a bingle with one of them, occasionally a child got bitten or a dog hurt by a car. Even 25 years ago back in Switzerland our dog Ajtano would go to work with my husband. He would roam the streets, spend time with strangers, steal sandwiches and come back when it was time to go home. He got picked up by well-meaning people occasionally and once by police. It was no big problem, no fines: it was a different time. I am not saying we should go back to the old times, but because dogs are not allowed anywhere without their humans, human-led socialisation has become very important. It also has become more difficult and time-consuming.

Part of the problem is our own expectations of our dogs, which are extremely and unfairly high. We bring dogs into our lives because we want dogs and then expect them not to behave like dogs. We expect them to fit in with our busy lifestyle and suburban housing density (e.g. being happy left alone in the backyard all day), forgetting that they are not really made for suburbia and that we *deliberately* bred them to be loyal and dependent on us. Most behaviours we consider 'bad' are natural and normal behaviours for dogs – and even more so for teenage dogs. They jump on people, they dig, they bark, they mouth and chew, they hump and they don't want to be alone! These behaviours are just unwanted *by us* because they are inconvenient *for us*.

Additionally, we want our dog to be a calm companion, but often do not take the time to create conditions that allow for calmness. We cannot expect them to be calm when they only see us briefly, between work and a social engagement in the evening and are otherwise left alone. This is unreasonable. We get dogs as companions, leave them home alone all day, and then ask them to leave us alone so we can decompress from our day of leaving them alone. For most dogs this is too big of an ask! For advice on how to teach, capture and promote calmness, see Chapter 7.

 In real life I meet a lot of teenage dogs who are bored out of their minds at home in the backyard or dogs who spend most of their day alone. They develop separation distress-related behaviours such as barking/howling and escape or destructive behaviours. They also become overly-attached and seek excessive attention as soon as their human is home.

Ultimately, it is not fair that we relegate our dog to the backyard away from us when they behave like dogs and we cannot expect them to cope with being left alone hours on end. Bushes and flowers in the backyard really don't make for interesting company. Wynne, the author of the book *Dog Is Love: Why and How Your Dog Loves You,* says in an interview[65] that 'We take it for granted that a dog can just be left and it'll be ok. This causes real distress to dogs.'

Putting our dog in the back yard can become a vicious cycle because we might find taking them out more challenging and every time we go out, our teenage dog behaves in a way we might find unacceptable or embarrassing. In the end we don't go out at all, hoping that once they are grown-up, they might miraculously become a well-adjusted and easy-going dog. With their life more restricted and a lot of time spent in the backyard, yard teenage dogs face a rapid process of 'de-socialisation' and the previously well-adjusted puppy now finds the world a scary place.

Because we live in cities with 9-5 desk jobs, we are spending less-and-less time at home with our dog and they are left without a job to do. This means that they don't have the opportunity to express the part of themselves that their breed/species was originally selected for (e.g. hunting, herding, search-and-rescue, protection), and it is our responsibility to provide them the chance to keep busy with different sorts of 'jobs'. These jobs keep them engaged and happy to be part of our human world (see Section 8.2.1). There are many different options, but keep in mind they all require us to go out of our way to spend quality time with our dog and adjust our lives accordingly; although dogs are legally living in our human world, that doesn't mean we don't have to personally adjust to sharing and creating a multispecies household.

In addition to giving our dogs jobs, proper socialisation into the societies we live in is the most important task when raising a well-adjusted dog who can cope with our modern world. When we get a puppy, we need to know what they will have to do later in life: do they need to board, go on holidays, go to the groomer, attend day care, go out with a dog walker, go to the coffee shop, participate in a dog sport, etc.? All these things should be introduced early – if possible, before six months of age – because they are the sorts of social challenges for which we must prepare our teenage and mature dog.

Odin and Chester don't need to be perfect, but they do need to perceive other humans and dogs as safe to approach and interact with. Both these dogs are still young and eventually they will learn not to jump up on people, but for now they are working on feeling comfortable in the presence of other dogs and humans and learning to accept leashes and harnesses. In time they will learn to sit instead of jumping up when greeting humans. Picture Jess Sandstrom.

6.2 Early socialisation

Breeders, foster carers and rescue volunteers play an important role in puppy socialisation. The most comprehensive resource on how to raise confident and outgoing puppies is 'Puppy Culture'[66]. This is a step-by-step program on how to successfully socialise puppies from birth.

Early handling is a must; puppies need to be handled gently and daily. They need to be socialised to a wide range of stimuli for living in a human world – most importantly: people and more people. Before they leave for their forever home, they should have met toddlers, children, teenagers, adults, older people and people in different outfits such as trades-people fluro vests, coats, umbrellas, people of different back-grounds, males, females, etc. Meeting the same people repeatedly (like the immediate family) is not socialisation, but, rather, habituation. Our puppies need to meet other friendly animals and get used to different noises (there are a lot of apps and noise CDs available for this purpose[67]). We can create a positive association with fun play, interaction, tasty treats, cuddles and pats (see Section 9.1.2).

Most puppies will be living in a family home, so it makes sense that they are born in a home and not in a kennel. They need to spend their first eight weeks in a home where they are exposed to the normal noises and coming-and-goings of a busy household. I would only ever buy a puppy who was raised in a family home. A puppy who was born and raised in a kennel environment will have much more difficulties in adjusting to living in a family environment. Think, for example, of the difference between a child's ability to cope in a family environment when they were born into one versus being born and raised in an orphanage and then transported into a family home.

Beyond exposure to people, part of the benefit of being raised in a family home comes in the form of exposure and positive association with an enriched environment. Puppies need environmental socialisation to toys, food-dispensing puzzles, tunnels, objects and different sorts of surfaces to step, play and balance on, etc. Our puppies need to be able to freely explore, interact, manipulate and investigate their surroundings in their own time and at their own pace.

Puppies should also have made several car trips with a positive outcome (i.e. trips to the vet do not count), to reduce their fear of traveling in a car. For some puppies the car becomes a scary place because they only drove in a car when going to the vet or when leaving their first home. As most puppies will need to travel, puppy-raisers should make sure puppies experience car travels with their litter mates and mother before going to their new home. This will make it much easier for their new humans and the puppies.

Most humans (with the appropriate guidance) can socialise their puppies to people, surfaces, noises and environments, but who has access to other puppies of a similar age? Hardly anyone! A well-run puppy preschool is often the only place where a puppy can safely meet other puppies and practice appropriate body language. Puppy pre-schools are a great opportunity to socialise a puppy to a wide range of people and environments, especially since most puppies love to play. They need to learn to interact and meet other puppies of different sizes, temperaments and looks. They also need to be able to calm down in the presence of other puppies and ignore them. A puppy pre-school with carefully moderated off-leash interactions is the best place to socialise with other dogs. There is nothing wrong with doing more than one puppy class. It is also the place to set humans up for proper training and help with trouble shooting, since us humans have a lot to learn about interacting and communicating with our new friends.

Puppy pre-schools are safer than going to dog parks because the dog park is unpredictable and potentially dangerous for a puppy and should not be part of socialisation until puppies are at least six months old (see Section 6.4.2). An alternative to pre-school or dog parks that I also recommend is setting up play dates with people we meet at puppy class (because their dogs are a similar age) or with older, patient dogs. A good day care or puppy socialisation groups are another good way for additional dog-to-dog socialisation.

> **Training tip** Under no circumstances should you book your puppy into a class which does not let puppies play in carefully moderated off-leash interactions. I see too many young dogs who do not know how to interact with other dogs or fear other dogs because they have not learnt to play. This can quickly lead to aggression. Puppies need to learn to play to develop social skills. Three different skills need to be taught in a puppy class:
> - Appropriate play
> - Ignore other puppies and relax
> - Short meet-and-greets
>
> All of these skills are equally important and must be taught at the same time. Puppies cannot be calm and relaxed in the presence of other puppies if they are not allowed to meet and sometimes play.

Importantly, all socialisation must happen on our puppy's own terms and they must be able to make a choice (see Section 3.2.4). If our puppy decides not to approach a certain stimulus, then we need to accept that. There is nothing wrong with encouraging, but under no circumstances should the puppy be forced into an interaction. This freedom to explore on their own terms contributes to puppies being more inquisitive, better able to cope with stress and solve problems.

Just a quick word on so-called independence training for very young puppies: I see an ever-increasing number of dogs who are stressed or have separation anxiety when left alone. In my opinion, this is caused by leaving puppies alone too early in their development. We are told that puppies need to learn to be alone, yet the only reason puppies need to learn to be alone early is 'convenience' – for the humans, not the dogs. We have busy lives; we get a puppy and then the puppy needs to learn to spend most of the time alone at home, starting at the age of eight weeks.

No one even considers teaching a human baby or toddler to be alone and no one worries they will develop separation anxiety if we do not leave them alone at an early age. Everyone will tell you just the opposite; children should not be left alone and they will learn to be alone once they are mature enough. The same goes for our dogs: they will learn to be alone when they are mature enough. While puppies need to learn to self-sooth, they should not just be left to cry; they need to be reassured if they get stressed.

 In real life I do not leave my dogs alone until they are about 12 months old. Until then they have the company of either an older dog or a human. It is like a miracle once they are around a year old, they can stay home alone without previous independence training. I am aware that not everyone can do this, but I think we need to seriously reconsider if getting a puppy is the right decision for someone who works full time, has a busy social life and is not willing to make changes for the puppy's sake.

6.3 Continual, and teenage, socialisation

Let's assume we did all the early socialisation and now our pup is a stroppy, moody teenager. Despite the window of opportunity closing, we must keep up our socialisation efforts, so the 'socialisation muscle' stays strong, fit and healthy in our teenage dogs. We will need to expose our teenage dog to new experiences on an ongoing basis and in a positive way. This can be a bit of an uphill battle because, as we know, the brain of our teenage dog relies on the limbic system to make decisions and is not always processing information correctly (see Section 2.2). They will go through secondary fear phases and might react intensely, 'over the top' and without much self-control to social interactions. It is our job to adjust appropriately. This means there will be times where we must be careful and manage the environment closely (see Section 9.4) and actively work to create positive associations (see Section 9.1.2). So, don't fret if you just got a teenage dog from a rescue or a breeder. Socialisation can be done at this stage and the same puppy-socialisation principles apply – it just needs a bit more planning and a more systematic approach.

In terms of socialising our teenage dog to the human world, we start by ensuring they have settled into their new home. Then, we take them out to different places and create positive associations. Because the brain is at the teenage developmental stage, they will need more gradual exposure. Being too close to a skateboard, a bike, a big dog or a bus could trigger lunging and barking (they might think there is a boogie man out there to get them). This means we stay further away and only gradually decrease distance while feeding treats (i.e. associating a potentially scary stimulus positive by using treats; see Section 9.1.2). As with puppies, we don't force our teenage dog to go closer than what they are offering themselves. We stay at a distance where our dog feels safe and remains calm. Once they have been gradually exposed to a few environments, we should aim to take them (up to at least 18 months of age) to new and different places a couple of times a week; a different coffee shop, a different shopping strip or a new track. Once they are over 18 months, we should take them to a new place or for a new experience as often as we can – just to make sure!

Regarding ongoing socialisation with other dogs or remedial socialisation with rescue dogs, we can set up play dates with our friends' dogs if they are stable and friendly. It often is best to take them for on-leash walks first, with short meet-and-greets on leash (see Section 9.8.4) but mostly walking, sniffing and exploring together so they get used to each other's company while remaining calm. I recommend meeting on neutral territory; most dogs are more relaxed there than when meeting at home. Once they know each other, we can go to a fenced area (or if the stable dog accepts other dogs in their yard that can work, too). We then have the stable, calm dog off-leash first and see if they want to interact with the rambunctious teenager. If they approach and invite play then we can try to have both dogs off-leash. If that works, we then extend their circle of friends and eventually go to the off-leash area to meet unknown dogs. When going to the off-leash area it helps to go at a similar time and meet the same dogs and humans (at least initially) so our teenager meets familiar dogs before being challenged with meeting several strangers at once.

While we create a positive association with other people and dogs, it does not mean that our teenage dog needs to greet everyone as a long-lost friend. But we do need them to perceive the world as a positive and safe place. This means they can ignore a lot of things but still have a positive attitude and feel safe in the presence of a variety of stimuli. Ongoing socialisation, despite the frustration, seemingly forgotten training and the patience required, is essential to keep the brain developing, in addition to keeping channels of communication open. While it might seem that our dog has forgotten everything, this is also the time when they learn a lot of new things. New pathways are developing in the brain and the more we train in a positive way the more we are developing appropriate patterns and channels in the brain for later in life (see Section 2.2.2).

Training tip Attending a teenage dog–training class can be invaluable in getting help with training. It helps to gain perspective and realise that you are not alone but that other people have very similar problems. It is also an opportunity to socialise and keep up the motivation for training.

6.4 Problematic socialisation

Behaviour is never stable and it always changes, sometimes for the better and sometimes for the worse. While teenage dogs often enjoy social time they also go through a phase where they can become a bit 'stroppy' (human parents: sound familiar?) with other dogs in off-leash situations. A previously well-socialised and easy-going dog may suddenly become a bully. Their body language towards other dogs is more assertive, they might get into scraps and not take *no* for an answer. One reason for this is the lack of self-control, given that the 'brakes' in their brain have not developed yet and they are still trying to figure out what works and what does not work in a social context (see Section 2.2).

It is common for adolescent dogs to posture, stare, intrude into other dogs' space, growl, snap and sometimes fight. After all, they are dogs and do not air their grievances by writing letters to the editor. Air-snapping and growling are a normal part of communication, indicating that our dog wants more space. These are also precursors for more assertive displays such as lunging or biting. We should never punish our dog for growling (lest they start suppressing the warning and go straight to biting) but, rather, take this as information and maybe go slower and give them more time and space to get used to the situations they find challenging. If no one is hurt then it is just part of growing up; if another dog gets hurt or if our dog keeps getting into fights (even if no one is hurt) we need to act urgently and contact a qualified trainer to work through this. While it is very upsetting for us, it is often a lack of confidence in the teenage dog that causes this behaviour.

When dealing with stroppy teenage dogs, we must keep our expectations realistic. It is unfair to expect our dog to get along with every other dog they meet. At the age of about two to three years they have their friends and social group they prefer to interact with (see Section 2.2.5). But they still need to be able to cope with unfamiliar dogs by either ignoring them or walking away after a short meet-and-greet. Unfortunately, the first altercation with another dog is often the end of ongoing socialisation for teenage dogs and the beginning of a vicious cycle of them meeting fewer-and-fewer unfamiliar dogs and their reaction becoming more-and-more inappropriate. This is why socialisation is a lifelong process.

6.4.1 On-leash socialisation

When it comes to meeting other dogs on-leash, two behaviours should be taught: one is *heel* (which means keep walking and ignore the other dog) and the other one is *say-hello* (see Sections 9.8.3 and 9.8.4). *Say-hello* is a short meet-and-greet – about three seconds. *Say-hello* is different from allowing dogs to play on-leash.

On-leash play is inappropriate for several reasons. The main one is that dogs cannot display appropriate body language because they are restricted by the leash. They cannot approach sideways or from behind and they cannot move away if they feel trapped. On-leash greetings are often head-on and some dogs find this challenging and rude, especially emotional teenage dogs. If dogs meet off-leash, they will go to the rear end or approach from the side. On-leash they cannot do that and might end up in a tangle. This often leads to on-leash altercations and can, in the long run, create leash reactivity. Additionally, allowing interactions on-leash creates the expectation in our teenage dog that they can interact with every dog they meet. That is not possible because some dogs are not social and do not want to meet other dogs, especially an exuberant teenager. It also leads to humans being dragged down the road attached to a leash, to meet every dog in view.

By teaching dogs that it is ok to ignore others, we are communicating to them that not everyone needs to be treated like a long-lost friend. We also teach that while there are places and times for play and interaction (off-leash), there are times when that isn't our goal (on-leash). Most dogs understand that if we are consistent. The leash then becomes a reliable predictor and communicator of the expected behaviours: either *heel* (for unknown dogs) or *say-hello* (for known dogs), but not play. See Section 9.8.3 for a step-by-step guide on how to teach appropriate behaviours associated with the leash.

 In real life I personally ask my dogs to *heel* (and ignore the other dog) when meeting other unknown dogs. This is safe and lets my dogs know that we are not meeting other dogs when on-leash. It is a different situation when we meet dogs and people we know. My dogs will *say-hello* to their dog friends if we meet them on-leash. When dogs know each other, they are more comfortable in close proximity and have less issues with being constrained or meeting one another head-on.

6.4.2 Dog parks

The dog park is a relatively new concept and probably born from the changing social role of dogs over the last 50 years (see Section 6.1). Along with dogs becoming more-and-more regulated, there are also less-and-less public spaces for them to move freely. One dog-friendly public space is the dog park. California introduced the first dog park in 1979 and Australia has had them for about 30 years now.

These days it seems like dog parks are the most popular – and often only – place for dogs and people feel every dog must go. Ideally, the dog park is a place where dogs are playing nicely with each other, their humans are supervising closely, occasionally calling their dogs back, reinforcing, then asking for a *sit*, providing another reinforcer and letting them go again. Things are rather calm and relaxed, with low arousal levels.

However, contrary to common beliefs and this ideal goal, the off-leash dog park is not always the best place to socialise our dogs, as there are too many things that can go wrong and cause long-term psychological damage. The dog park is a place for well-socialised dogs who are resilient enough to bounce back when something goes wrong. In my experience only about 20% of dogs enjoy the dog park experience, 30% will cope and do their own thing as long as the other dogs leave them alone – but 50% of the dogs in the park are saying loud and clear: *get me out of here – this is no fun!* These dogs will avoid other dogs as much as they can, sniff intently, turn their heads away, lick their lips and show more displacement behaviours (see Section 3.2.3 for more information on body language). If the other dogs do not understand, these dogs might growl, bark, lunge and – if necessary – bite. The main problem with dog parks is that is a confined area where too many dogs try to get along with each other. By taking our dog to dog parks, we make them meet unknown dogs on an ongoing basis and expect them to play with strangers (or at least tolerate them).

While teenage dogs need off-leash time and to be able to interact with other dogs during this development phase, the dog park is fraught with danger. It does not take too many bad experiences for our previously well-socialised and happy-go-lucky dog to become scared. One bad incident with an adult dog annoyed with a teenager in their face can cause a lot of damage!

 In real life Just another day at the off-leash dog park: There is Mum, three kids and their exuberant six-month-old Labrador. He is jumping in the other dogs' faces while Mum shouts 'he is friendly and just wants to play!' The other dogs try to run but there is no escape. Ill-Advised Dog Trainer is there with a dog scared of other dogs. The fearful dog is trying to increase distance and avoid the other dogs, but he cannot escape because he is on-leash (a bad idea in the first place in an off-leash park). Dog Trainer explains that he 'needs to get used to it'. The dog is showing a lot of stress signs but no one takes note until he lunges, then he gets yelled at and jerked on the leash. Dog Trainer is looking rather confused about where this aggression originated. Meanwhile, Hipster is on the phone and his French bulldog is trying to hump a Great Dane. Everyone laughs and thinks it is very funny. The bulldog loves the attention and keeps going. A Jack Russell has disappeared into the bushes and has no intention of coming back. These are typical, interrelated dramas that are all happening in a confined space and point to the difficulty of creating a safe space for our teenage dog in these boisterous parks.

There are some groups of dogs who should not go to the off-leash area, given their vulnerable status or their personality traits. The obvious ones include unvaccinated puppies or, really, puppies in general; females in season; sick or old dogs; and reactive or aggressive dogs. Dogs who do not enjoy other dogs' company and are fearful or nervous around them should not be forced to engage in this socially-artificial environment. Very small dogs are at risk because not all big dogs have learnt to play appropriately with little dogs. Also, bigger dogs can mistake little fluffy dogs in the distance for rabbits and chase them, which might not end well. Entire males are also not the best candidates here in Australia; because there are so few entire dogs, there is anecdotal evidence that they get 'picked on' by other dogs. Some humans also have trouble accepting entire dogs in off-leash parks.

So, who then makes a good candidate? The answer is: dogs who are well-socialised and resilient and enjoy the company of other (unknown) dogs. This means we need to know how to read their body language, personality and emotional stability so we can make good choices for what *they* want. The dog park is a place for socialised dogs to meet other socialised dogs, not a place for unsocialised dogs to learn how to be social. Well-socialised and trained teenage dogs from around six months to two years are often good candidates for the off-leash dog park because they enjoy meeting other dogs and will play with unknown dogs. Mature dogs are less likely to enjoy the dog park as they prefer to socialise within their own circles of friends.

Once we've decided our dog might like a visit to the local dog park, we need to manage the visit carefully. We should only take our well-socialised teenage dog to safe, fenced areas at times when there are only a few other dogs around and it isn't too busy, preferably dogs of appropriate size and temperament. Check out the other users and the other dogs before going into a dog park, to check for potential bullies and how attentive the humans are to the bullying. Keeping it short, maybe 10-20 minutes, carefully watching our dog's body language and calling them back to us when it gets too boisterous will help make it a positive experience. If our dog does not like to share their toys, we need to leave the toys at home.

The choice of dog park is another important consideration. A park that has engaging features (water access, trees, play equipment and not just an empty space) is better because our dogs can do other things than just playing with each other. These features also provide incentive for sniffing, marking and calmer activities such as exploring. Fencing is important as it provides a security blanket if our dog gets a bit excited and doesn't want to come back.

If we scout out all these details and deem it safe, we can take our teenage dog into the park. We must stay aware of our dog's comfort and enjoyment while there, in addition to any signs that they may start being stroppy or bullying others. If a dog gets bullied, both of their humans should intervene and redirect their dogs to more appropriate playmates. The line between bullying and playing can be difficult to discern. Most people do not recognise what counts as 'good play'. Good play ebbs and flows, which means the dog take turns: one dog chases another, then they switch; one is on top, then the other one is. There is disengagement and engagement; play behaviours such as play bow, eye-flashing, 'bouncy' movements are displayed and there is the occasional lull in the activity. If it is too one-sided or too rough, the humans should interrupt and regroup (see Section 9.3).

Another way of looking at it is using the MARS acronym[68]: meta-signals, activity-shift, role-reversal and self-handicapping. *Meta-signalling* is a communication to the play partner that they are just playing and the behaviour should not be interpreted as aggressive. Meta-signals include play bows, bouncy movements, eye-flashing and exaggerated motions. *Activity-shift* means that there are times of high activity and then times where the activity slows down. They might even lie down and then start again. *Role-reversal* is the change of who chases, who is on top and who bites. In good play the role changes frequently. *Self-handicapping* happens when the bigger or stronger dog limits the use of their strengths by lying down and slowing movement (i.e. deliberately handicapping themselves to ensure the play continues). Paying attention to these behaviour patterns will help humans to recognise when play turns into bullying or becomes aggressive.

If we watch our dog's and other dogs' body language, we will recognise the signs that play is getting out of control: raised hackles, ears are back and down, one-sided interaction, no pausing, no play bows and raised intensity (to name a few). As with some people, some dogs just do not get along, and they start staring or eyeballing each other immediately upon meeting. They might move slowly, circle each other or show early signs of stress. When one dog puts their head on another dog's shoulder, we have most likely missed a lot of communication and stress signs going on between these two dogs. However, if we watch closely, we may see early signs of stress through displacement behaviours like lip-licking or yawning, turning away or trying to get away, even before we see an increase in the intensity. Watch for play bows, raised paws, play face, ebb and flow and relaxed bodies to make sure all is going well. Be aware that a wagging tail does not necessarily mean a happy dog. Too often we assume a wagging tail means all is good, however if the tail is wagging frantically and in a raised position it can indicate high arousal. A lowered tail, waging gently and a generally relaxed body indicates a relaxed dog, ready to play.

Letting dogs run unsupervised and un-managed while we get caught up in conversation or are on the phone is a recipe for a disaster; this is because it is better to intervene early and calmly by calling their name, asking them to come to us and reinforce (see Section 9.3) *before* the behaviour escalates into an emergency. If we don't closely supervise, when we do finally notice our dog's stress or aggression, we might panic, run over, grab and reprimand our dog. This will most likely make it worse because our dog is now associating the other dog with even more negative events and the emotions they trigger (see Section 4.5). Another risk is that our dog generalises the bad experience to a person nearby, the location or a sound. They are now not only scared of the other dog but potentially of a lot of other things, too. What we should do in this situation is immediately call our dog back to us and reinforce them. Then we need to redirect our dog to another playmate or if they are stressed and aroused, we might just head off for a nice on-leash walk.

Overall, we should keep arousal levels low at the dog park. If our dog gets excited when we approach the dog park, we need to make sure we calm them down with some fun training before they can play with their mates. Once in the park, the best way to keep arousal levels low is to keep play sessions short, interrupt play when they get too excited and call them back. When they *come,* we need to reinforce generously, play with them, calm things down and then let them go again.

There are a lot of lovely, happy, completely normal and well-socialised dogs who do not cope with the dog park and do not want to go there. It is like with humans; some are extroverts and some are introverts and there is nothing wrong with either. As their human, we should respect this and look for alternative ways of having a good time with our dog if they are introverts. A good alternative is going for walks with a group of dog friends and having a play at the end. Or, we could do a fun agility class or any other dog sport where dogs meet in a social setting without having to directly play with one another if they do not feel like it. A well-run day care where they meet their friends is another option. I also recommend on-leash walks in a range of places like parks, beaches, forests and occasionally a completely new place. Dogs on-leash are allowed in many places, city or country.

Eddy and Coco having an off-leash run. Despite the challenges for teenage dogs at the dog park, it is often the only place where they can run and enjoy some canine company. If well-managed and supervised it can be a lot of fun! Picture Le Hammer.

6.4.3 Inappropriate social exposure

As described in terms of overwhelming social experiences at dog parks, *inappropriate* social exposure can lead to a fearful dog. If we are not careful, we might create (un)intentional negative social associations. This means we are not socialising at the dog's pace and we are putting them into situation where they cannot cope. Typical situations for this are things like: Christmas parties, where our dog or the puppy is left unsupervised to deal with a lot of people and children they are not use to; taking them to a busy coffee shop before having practiced at less-busy places; or taking them to the dog park where they meet too many boisterous dogs before having had enough small-scale positive interactions and a chance to develop resilience.

 In real life Imagine this scenario: a well-meaning mum takes her brand-new puppy to see her daughter play soccer. She pops the leash on and goes to the park. Her daughter's entire team runs up to the puppy and tries to pat the pup. The puppy might feel trapped but the leash prevents them from backing off. They might get really scared by this overwhelming experience. The puppy now has a bad association with the lead, open space, girls of a certain age, screaming children and more. A far better method would be to start slower with the social interactions: introduce the puppy to one or two of her daughter's friends first at home, then take the puppy to the park when there is no one there, then invite a few friends over and have a small party, then go to the park when the girls train and then maybe she can take the puppy to a real, high-excitement soccer game. The same applies for new rescue dogs – do not rush it!

The vet is another example of a problematic social situation; this is often a place where our dog gets poked, handled and restrained. Our dog might get scared in this new environment. If they are not able to form a positive association with the vet before their first vaccination, we might create a life-long problem. Therefore, it is important to take our puppy in for social visits a few times before something 'bad' like an injection happens (see Section 9.8.6). Once they have formed a positive association, they cope better and often maintain a positive attitude despite the sometimes painful treatment. This is called *latent inhibition* and can be very useful in preventing fear learning (see Section 4.5). We need to make sure that we are using a vet who is aware of these problems and uses the least-invasive procedures possible. For example, a cream that numbs the skin where the injection is made can prevent pain and goes a long way to help our pup to stay positive. It is worthwhile checking which vet in your area is certified as Fear-Free[69]. While this is an American initiative, there are fear-free vets in Australia and other parts of the world.

6.5 Summary

Dogs need to learn to exist in our human worlds, including car trips, coffee shops, walks, dog parks, vet clinics or being left alone (and self-soothing). Because of the changes in our lived environment and our expectations for dogs, socialisation has become more difficult, time-consuming and more important. In order to learn social expectations, dogs need to be socialised early – and it needs to be an ongoing process as they become teenagers and then mature adults. However, even if a rescue dog missed part of their socialisation as a puppy, we still can successfully socialise teenage dogs. There are some common, difficult situations when socialising our teenage dogs, including on-leash meetings, dog parks and rushing or overwhelming them with new situations. We can never socialise to everything but well-socialised dogs will take new challenges in their stride. Socialisation is well worth the effort because a confident and well-adjusted dog is easier to live with for us and our dogs will have a better life because they can go places with us.

Chapter 7
Changing job descriptions – Is calm just another behaviour?

In the last few decades, we have changed the job descriptions for our dogs, but somewhere along the line we forgot to tell them! Until maybe 20 years ago we wanted our dogs to bark at 'intruders'; this was one of the main reasons for keeping dogs in the first place. Now we ask them to stay calm all the time – even when Jehovah's Witnesses knock at the boundary of their territory or if the plumber rushes through the front door to get to a flooded bathroom. We want them to be calm when visitors come over, when we have Christmas dinner, when we go to the dog park and – ironically – when we yell at them to be calm. It seems we want them to be calm – full stop. But this is not how dogs are. Because of this change in the job description, our dog needs to learn to be calm in a way that is counter to their nature and counter to the way we have selected dogs for breeding over the last few centuries.

For most dogs 'being calm' does not come naturally and it is one of the more difficult behaviours to teach. Being calm is also not the same as a cued *sit-stay* or *down-stay*. Without becoming too airy-fairy, calm is not just the absence of arousal, or a heightened state of alert or stress, nor is it an emotional 'shut down'. For dogs, calm means that they are content, happy and relaxed. They can lie on their bed and watch the world go by without barking at every noise or thing that moves. Calm is a state of mind or a concept (see Section 3.1.1).

As those with human children and teenagers, or anyone who has dabbled in meditation, can tell you, calm can be a difficult concept. It is normal for puppies to only have two speeds: One is *go-go-go* and the other is *crash-and-go-to-sleep*. For very young puppies, calm is not really on the agenda. Calm is even more difficult for teenage dogs. For dogs who have no job and not enough company, calm is an impossible state of mind. The teenage phase is the age where dogs most need a job because their brain is developing, synapses are growing, they are fit, curious and have a lot of stamina. If we do not provide outlets for their energy and cater to their needs (see Section 8.2), they cannot be calm.

We can (and should) start teaching relaxation at a young age. Like everything else, teaching calm needs to be age specific; for puppies a few minutes of a relaxing massage or that two-second *sit-stay* might be all we can expect. For teenage dogs it may mean being calmly on their bed while we have dinner or resting on a mat at the coffee shop (however, make sure to order take-away at the coffee shop just in case we need to leave because our mat training was not as advanced as we thought!).

Overall, there are a lot of different ways to provide incentive and an environment that promotes calm. The benefits are a reduction in unwanted behaviours like barking and chewing in addition to a calmer, more rewarding relationship with us. There are also a lot of different protocols to teach calm. In my experience, it is best to use a holistic approach. This means providing appropriate stimulation and company, teaching impulse control, capturing calm, addressing barking and promote chewing. If our dog cannot be calm around certain stimuli, then we need to counter-condition them to that stimuli.

7.1 Prerequisites for teaching calm

The first (and probably most important) step to giving our dogs time to be calm is to provide adequate outlets for our dog's energy and cater to their social need for companionship (see Section 8.2). All dogs – but especially teenage dogs – need physical exercise, brain stimulation and company. If these needs are not met, we cannot expect them to be calm. You can probably relate: do you feel calm if you have had nothing to do and no one to talk to all day? If you've just sat on the couch and zoned out? Or do you feel calm in the lulls between those stimulating and enriching goals and encounters?

This is supported by research into stress and learning; we need an optimal level of challenge to stay engaged (see Section 4.5). Dogs who have an appropriate level of stimulation are better able to process information and cope (see Section 8.2). For example, when food enrichment toys were provided to laboratory dogs, there was a trend for dogs with toys to show fewer stereotyped behaviours (often associated with stress and boredom) and less barking[70]. They were, essentially, calmer when they had a food puzzle to concentrate on.

Fortunately, there are now more-and-more workplaces that will allow dogs to accompany their humans to the office, in addition to more opportunities to work from home for at least for part of the working week. For the sake of our teenage dog, I would recommend these options, if possible. Another option is to use a good day-care centre or engage a reliable dog walker. These options will help our dogs to be calmer when home because their needs for company are met and they spend less time alone.

Getting a second dog is another approach to encouraging calmness. Most dogs love the company of another dog and it can help them feeling less lonely when their humans are at work. However, the introduction of another dog can be difficult and time consuming and must be done carefully[71]. It can also be more work if the dogs are at completely different life stages and have different exercise and socialisation needs. It is certainly more expensive having two dogs. I think it works best if the dogs are two to three years apart in age.

So, if we find our dog is unable to calm down, we should first ask whether we have provided sufficient company, stimulation, enrichment, exercise and outings, since these are required 'non-calm' activities that help to be able to be 'calm'.

7.2 Teach impulse control

Impulse control means our dog can delay a reaction to an exciting (or scary) stimulus and think about it before reacting. Teenage dogs, with their developing brains, tend to (re)act first and then think (see Chapter 2). That is what we see when they jump all over us or visitors or bark at a 'scary' backpack on the floor. If we teach them alternative behaviours (e.g. *watch-me*, Doggy-Zen and *hand-touch*) or stationary behaviours (e.g. *wait* and *lie-down*), we are able to prevent the act first and allow a few seconds for processing the information before they react. It is our responsibility to ensure that our teenage dogs have these 'focus' behaviours in their repertoire and that they are well trained so they can be successful even in the face of distractions or scary stimuli. Ideally, once they have learnt these behaviours, they will look to us for guidance when they encounter something scary or exciting. This allows them to access a reinforcer by calming down, offering a more appropriate behaviour and therefore reduce the over-the-top reaction.

Chillax cool, calm and collected. His ears and eyes are in a neutral position, his brows are smooth, his mouth is half open, he is breathing calmly, looking at something with interest but staying seated. Picture Barbara Hodel.

7.3 Capturing calm

Interestingly, most humans miss their dog's calm behaviour. A typical scenario is our dog is calm on their bed and is ignored while we surf the web or watch TV. However, as soon as they get up, we react. Even if our dog is getting a negative reaction, it is still reinforcing. In the teenage dog world, any attention is better than no attention. By mistake, the getting up is reinforced while the calm is ignored. This tells the dog being calm is not worth doing.

We need to change our approach and 'capture calm' (see Section 5.2 on capturing as a form of positive reinforcement training). This should be a major part of our relaxation protocol and comes about through prolonged 'down time' together (another reason it is important to have our dogs inside the home with us; see Section 3.2.1). It is also training us humans to pay more attention to our dogs and acknowledge calm (see Section 5.3).

When we see our dog in a relaxed state of mind, we let them know by telling them in a low and gentle voice that they are a *good dog*. We do not use treats or move towards them – otherwise they might go back into working mode. It's that simple; just acknowledge they are doing something we approve of and then go right back to what we were doing!

7.4 Chewing promotes calm

We often forget that dogs like to chase, dissect, chew and eat a variety of things, even after the teething phase is over. A diet based on dry food does not address their need for chewing. This can lead to dogs who chew a lot of inappropriate, non-digestible things like furniture, rugs, humans, random plants, etc.; young dogs will chew indiscriminately if not taught otherwise.

Chewing is often a response to stress; so, we should provide our dog with a chewing option when we notice the tell-tale signs of discomfort (see Section 3.2.3). In addition to being stress-relief, chewing also helps keep dogs to calm (think of how you reach for a chewing gum when you are stressed). Dogs chew to help them cope with boredom, loneliness, stress, frustration and even anxiety. This is because the act of chewing triggers the release of endorphins, and thus chewing 'is a tool that the dog has at his disposal in order to "self-medicate" for anxiety and stress'[72]. These are the reasons why we can use chews when we leave our dogs home alone, when visitors come to the house or when we are getting them used to storms or thunder – it gives them a way of coping. Chews can also be used to teach a stationary mat behaviour, making the early learning stages easier (see Section 9.8.1 for tips on mat training). Another side-effect of good chewing habit is that dogs who chew appropriately may need less dental work.

Therefore, having a variety of chews ready to use might just save your Persian rug or expensive hearing aids. If you feed raw appropriate bones, that is great. The best practice is to feed non-weight bearing bones – for example chicken wings, lamb necks or brisket bones. Toys specifically designed to withstand chewing can make good chewing choices, too, and may help our favourite pair of shoes or the pot plant we got as a wedding gift to survive our teenage dog. Food-dispensing toys are another good option and pet shops are full of dehydrated long-lasting treats that can go in these toys. I recommend feeding a bit less of their daily ration and make chews a part of their daily food intake.

However, as with creating enrichment, it isn't necessary to spend a fortune at the pet store to keep our dogs chewing! Some dogs take a liking to wooden sticks straight out of the garden (not the treated ones from building sites) and that is a free and readily-available chew toy alternative (just check for splinters!). Many of the plastic containers for yoghurts, pizza boxes, cardboard rolls, etc. make great chew toys. As with everything new, we need to make sure and supervise to ensure our dogs are ok.

Indi obviously needed something to chew. If we do not provide appropriate chew options such as toys or edible bones, they will chew whatever is there! Picture Grazia Pecoraro.

In real life A family in our teenage dog training class said that they were not able to eat their dinner in peace because their dog was not settling down, kept begging for food at the table or, if put outside, scratched at the door. They believed the dog should not be fed before them to make sure she knew her place in the household (an outdated idea based on the belief that dogs are pack animals and form strict hierarchies, and they need a human as the 'alpha'; see Section 3.1.2). I recommended to this family to provide their dog's dinner in a food-dispensing toy and some chews to keep her busy during mealtimes. They could use the food-dispensing toys in the yard and the chews to start mat training. When I asked the following week how they were going, they reported that the problem was solved. The dog was fed before dinner and then kept busy with a recreational bone during dinner time on her bed.

7.5 Why do they bark?

Barking is a normal behaviour for many dogs, but obviously not a desirable one in densely-populated areas. It is annoying; our neighbours might have complained personally or through council. Alternatively, if we need to leave our teenage dog home alone during the day, we might not even know that they are distressed and barking, in which case it is worthwhile talking to our neighbours to find out if they bark excessively or even howl when we are gone.

We are often looking for a quick fix to barking. Highly-aversive tools such as citronella, rattle cans and other unpleasant devices such as high-pitched noises and shock collars (to name a few) promise just that: a quick fix. It is rather scary how easily we resort to punishment just because it is easiest for us – at best doing something unpleasant and at worst something painful and scary to our dog. There is no need for it, and they aren't going to make the situation any better. In fact, the fallouts can be severe, and just 'hitting them over the head' could make the situation much, much worse. If dogs bark excessively, we need to figure out *why* and address the underlying *cause* of the problem, not just the *symptom*. This will allow them to feel calmer; we are addressing their needs, not just their behaviours (see Section 4.6).

In real life On our morning walks we see a lot of barking dogs behind fences but the behaviour of two dogs we encountered just did not make sense. Barking at dogs/people who go past properties is rather normal, especially for dogs who do not get enough mental and physical exercise. But these two did not just bark – they seemed to be in panicked, frenzied mode. I watched them for a bit longer. There is only one thing that creates this kind of panic and that is the use of an aversive tool such as a citronella or shock collar. Another time when I walked past the same house, my suspicion was confirmed when I heard the human yelling: 'Get up here or I will get the collar out!' I do not know if they use a citronella or a shock collar but both collars work with pain as a positive punishment, and it explains the behaviour of these two stressed-out dogs. The use of punishment can have severe side-effects and, in this case, it not only made the barking worse but the dogs are now extremely scared of dogs and people going past. They do not know what triggers the citronella/shock and have made the wrong association. They probably think the people or dogs going past trigger the pain, and so they now interpret other dogs and people as scary and dangerous.

Often dogs have their own very valid reasons to bark and we need to acknowledge that. As mentioned earlier, we have bred dogs to let us know when there are 'intruders' at the door and we need to accept that they bark in that situation. The same goes for our neighbour's cat on the fence or the possum that comes out at night. Teaching a *quiet* cue (see Section 9.7.7) will solve these problems without us engaging in a shouting match.

Beyond this normal communicative or excited barking, there are at least two other main reasons for barking: boredom and feeling unsafe outside or alone (including separation distress). Teenage dogs often find their voice when their increased exercise requirements are not met and they are bored. If we need to leave our dog home alone, we must make sure that they go out for a good walk before we leave. We need to provide both training and aerobic exercise (for both species!) while we are out on our walk. We should then leave their breakfast in a food-dispensing toy and have additional mind games ready for them when they get bored (see Section 8.2.1).

Most dogs feel safer – and calmer – if they have access to the inside living areas throughout the day. A dog door might make all the difference. I am aware that a lot of humans are reluctant to let their dogs inside if they are not home. However, it is important to give our dogs access to a safe place. Most dogs will prefer the living area over a kennel, probably because living areas are safe, family spaces while kennels can end up being used for punishment or isolation. I have met countless humans who bought a dog kennel only to find out their dog never used it. Providing access to the inside of the house and their humans (when they are home) will reduce barking and is one of the easiest ways to address a barking problem. Dogs who feel safe and secure rarely bark.

If the barking is caused by separation distress, we need to figure out first if it is a real separation anxiety or if it is simply a matter of them not having learnt to be alone. If we assume it is an anxiety, we might want to involve a veterinary behaviourist who can help with the diagnosis and decide if using medication would be appropriate. Alternatively, it may be that our dog has just not learnt to be on their own. Puppies and dogs do not take immediately to being left home alone, as they need to learn to enjoy their own company (note: there are people still working on learning this skill!).

Dogs can learn to enjoy their own company with the help of enrichment (see Section 8.2.1) and if we gradually get them used to the idea. This means settling them in when they first come to our home and then gradually getting them used to being home alone for longer and longer periods of time. For example, we can start by leaving them alone while we run a quick errand; if they do well with that, we can then start leaving them home alone for longer errands, eventually building up to a full workday.

 In real life When I talk to clients about giving their dogs access to the inside while they are at work, my suggestion is often met with doubt and hesitation. However, once we overcome our assumption that dogs like the backyard and give them access to their safe place in the house, they often calm down and the barking and howling stops. While it does not always work, it often does and is well-worth a trial. Plus, they are much safer: no open gates, no theft, no roaming. Sometimes circumstances such as rental arrangements make it difficult to provide a dog door. In these circumstances we have to look into alternatives such as making outdoor kennels or outdoor laundries as comfortable and relaxing as possible.

A thought on coming home: the advice to ignore our dog when coming home is still readily dispensed. It is not only heartbreaking but wrong and rude! If I come home and my husband does not say hello to me, then I know something is wrong. When coming home we need to say *hello* to our dogs and acknowledge them. They, and hopefully us, want to reconnect and make sure we are all ok. I recommend going down to their level and give them a hug (if they like it), a pat or play a game with them. Ignoring them will cause stress and will not make them calm down!

7.6 Calm via counter-conditioning

If our dog has already started barking at anything that moves, we will have to start by desensitising them to all these noises or movements. Desensitisation involves gradual exposure to a stimulus and counter-conditioning means teaching an alternative (incompatible) behaviour (see Section 9.1.2). This also means that we are dealing with the underlying issue and recontextualising it as a non-threat. We start this desensitisation counter-conditioning process at home. This means we are exposing our dogs to the stimulus that elicits their barking in a controlled way in order to change their perception (called respondent conditioning; see Section 9.1.2). To begin with, it helps if we manage the environment so there are not too many stimuli that will cause our dog to bark (e.g. people going past the house or dogs barking in the neighbourhood; see Section 9.4). In the early stages, especially when we are not at home, we can close the blinds to block the view or turn on the radio to block noises. We are trying to prevent rehearsal of the unwanted behaviour.

When we are at home, we start the desensitisation counter-conditioning process. We need to have small pieces of food ready (this can be their normal dry food) and every time the stimulus (or stimuli) that triggers a barking response appears (e.g. the neighbour going past the house), we give our dog a treat. Remember, we need to manipulate the environment so that our dog does not bark while they see the stimulus (see Section 9.4). This means we may move away from the window to create more distance, although we still need to stay close enough so that they see or hear the stimulus.

Ideally, we are working under threshold, meaning our dog does not bark. But even if they bark, we give them a treat. We are still in desensitising counter-conditioning mode, trying to change our dog's perception of the stimulus. The treat is contingent on the stimulus being present, not on their behaviour. Our dog gets treats as long as they can see the neighbour. Once the neighbour disappears, the treats cease. On a very basic level: the food makes our dog feel better and in time they will associate the neighbour with food and positive feelings or calmness. This may seem like magic, but really it is the magic of respondent conditioning. We are creating a positive emotional response when our dog sees the neighbour – something that was previously a stressful, bark-inducing event.

Once our dog is comfortable with the stimulus and anticipates the treat, we now add operant conditioning (teaching a behaviour and reinforcing it). As soon as our dog sees the neighbour, they will turn to us for the treat. We then ask them to *go-to-mat*, *mark* and *reinforce* (see Section 9.8.1). With enough repetitions, the neighbour will become the cue to *go-to-mat*. Ideally it then looks like this: our dog sees the neighbour going past the window, goes to their bed and gets a reinforcer. This means us humans need to be vigilant, have treats nearby and be aware when our dogs might bark. It may be helpful to use chews to gradually extend the time we ask our dog to stay on their bed. This does not happen overnight; we need to practice, but practice makes perfect. The end result is a calmer dog who doesn't bark at everything they see.

7.6 Summary

Dogs do no come pre-programmed to know what we want, so we must let them know – including teaching calm behaviours that often go unnoticed; this is especially important for teenage dogs. Our dogs can only reach this calm state of mind if their physical, mental and social needs are met and if they live in an environment that promotes and recognises calmness. With appropriate mental and physical stimulation, we can teach them to be calm and content even when home alone. Teaching calm requires a holistic approach; providing outlets for their energy and company for their social needs, teaching impulse control and preliminary behaviours such as Doggy Zen, *stay* and *go-to-mat* and capturing calm by gently acknowledging when they are on their bed and relaxing. If our dog is excessively barking or chewing when we leave during the day, they may be bored or distressed because they have not learnt to be home alone or calm. This can be helped by giving them access to a safe place inside when we are out and providing long-lasting and enriching chews that help to promote calmness. We can also use counter-conditioning to create more positive associations, which results in more time spent calm.

Chapter 8
The daily challenges – How to keep our sanity and help our teenage dog keep theirs

There are several daily challenges that can make us question our own sanity and ability to help our teenage dogs. The daily outings with teenage dogs can become more-and-more of a chore rather than a joy because of their emotional over-the-top reactions to some stimuli and forgotten training. It all becomes too hard to deal with for us on top of work, school, family, friends and community obligations. Some young dogs end up outside in the yard because this is easier than teaching them how to behave when inside with the family and providing daily walks, enrichment and training. Consequently, they go out less-and-less and become more-and-more reactive to novel stimuli. Additionally, they become incredibly bored and destructive and are often unable to settle (see Section 7.1).

I call these bored, backyard dogs *unemployed teenagers* who have now become *self-employed* – they have created jobs for themselves (parents with teenagers who have too much time on their hands and end up getting into trouble can probably relate). Digging up the yard, eating the pool lights and the outdoor furniture, barking at everything that moves, jumping on the children – these are attempts to keep their minds and bodies stimulated.

Let's look at some of the daily challenges we face – including startle responses, trigger stacking and behaviour chains. Then we'll explore how to keep everyone sane by providing enough and varied enrichment for our dog and making sure we take time to notice and appreciate what they are doing right without ignoring what they are doing wrong.

Indi sleeping next to his hole. If we do not provide enough mental and physical stimulation then teenage dogs will create their own jobs like digging up the backyard! Indi is proud of his hard day's work. Picture Grazia Pecoraro.

Training tip If you work full-time, have a busy social life and three children under the age of seven, please do not get a puppy or a dog. There are just not enough hours in a day. Puppies and dogs need – and deserve – at least two to three hours of quality time with their humans every day.

8.1 Daily challenges

All dogs, but especially teenagers, are prone to startle responses and trigger stacking and sometimes we make things worse by teaching a behaviour chain by mistake.

8.1.1 Startle response

A common situation with teenage dogs is that they get startled by unusual things (that is, things they consider unusual!), especially so during secondary fear phases. This can be a bag on the floor, a man with a hat, a traffic controller with a sign or a kid on a skateboard. Inanimate objects can be scary for dogs especially if they appear seemingly from nowhere in a familiar environment.

If our dog has already started barking the best option is to get out of that situation as quickly as possible and regroup at a distance where they can cope. If our dog is too excited or stressed it might be best to call it quits and take it easy for the rest of the day (see Section 4.5). If our dog can settle down, a re-socialisation session with the scary thing can help, but we need to make sure that they are coping and don't start barking again. This means we watch the scary thing from a safe distance and do not make our dog get too close (which can end up scaring them again). We reinforce for calmly looking at the scary thing (see Section 7.6).

We try to deal with our dogs' fears in a positive way: Reassuring our dog who is scared makes them feel safe and by providing reassurance, we are showing them that there is nothing to fear. This is contrary to common belief, which states that you can reinforce fear. For example, this antiquated idea suggests that if our dog is scared of thunder and we comfort them, they will learn that thunder is something to be scared of. This is incorrect; there is nothing wrong with calmly reassuring our dog. But staying relaxed will help them too; two startled and panicked individuals will not be helpful!

Training tip If our dog gets scared of something and barks or lunges at a stranger, a skateboard or has a run in with another dog, do not try to 'fix it' at that same moment. Our dog has already had a scare – their stress levels are elevated and their brain is not working properly (see Section 4.5). It is best to go somewhere else where our dog is comfortable but make a mental note of the thing that scared them. Reintroduce this stimulus carefully and in a controlled manner at a later stage. This means that once their stress levels are back to normal (this can take up to a week) let them have a look from a safe distance and associate the scary thing in a positive way, giving them treats. Technically we call this process desensitising and counter-conditioning (see Section 9.1.2). Do not flood them by asking too much too soon (*flooding* is a technical term for exposing a dog to a scary thing over a sustained period and at a high level of intensity, similar to the psychological concept of exposure therapy for phobias). For humans an example is if you were afraid of snakes you would be put into a snake pit. Imagine how scary that is and now it could make your fear worse! Patience is important here.

There are situations when letting our dog decide how to deal with a scary, startling thing is the best choice. If we are in a safe environment with no risk to our dog or someone else and they are only mildly scared, letting them figure it out for themselves can work well. Our dog can then make the decision to approach and check it out, walk away or maybe bark first and then investigate. They will go through a thought process and solve the problem.

This has a few advantages. Firstly, they learn how to cope in this situation by deciding for themselves. This is what we call 'concept training' – we do not just teach a specific behaviour such as *watch-me* but, rather, how to deal with a challenging situation (see Section 3.1.1). Secondly, it gives them choice – and choice is empowering and rewarding in-and-of itself (see Section 3.2.4). Thirdly, it will increase their confidence because they dealt with a mildly stressful situation and were successful. By providing a good, mild 'stress' (or enriching stimulation), their brains are kept more active and flexible (see Section 4.5)

 In real life In this case, the scary things my dogs were startled by were straw bales on the oval. I was at a fenced oval with both my dogs, mature-aged Shellbe and Chillax, the teenager. Both dogs had a look at the straw bales and, as expected, Chillax found them scary and started barking. We were alone on the oval; it was fenced and we had a lot of time. I did not use treats because I wanted him to think through this and decide what was the best option to deal with that scary thing. I wanted him to process the information without intervention from my side. He ran away, came back, had another look. He went closer and figured out the straw bale was not scary and was not going to eat him. He then weed on it. When he came back to me for a check-in, I gave him a few treats for the check-in. Note: This does not mean I do not use treats in similar situations if I am counter-conditioning and desensitising – it all depends on the specific situation.

8.1.2 Trigger stacking

There are days when it becomes all too much for our teenage dog. Their reaction towards something minor seems out of proportion and we don't understand what causes it. This is a case of *trigger stacking* or reaching a breaking point where we explode with frustration or anger from accumulated stress, in a way that is disproportionate and over-the-top.

The same goes for humans; some days are just too much. For humans trigger stacking looks like this: we get up in the morning and there is no milk in the fridge for our much-needed coffee; we then walk out of the door to go to work and our neighbour yells at us because the dog barked. When we reverse out of our driveway we almost get taken out by a truck. It is only 8:00 am, but we have had it. The next person who does something we do not like will cop it, regardless of how minor it is.

Dogs experience the same emotions. They might have had a bad night's sleep, a neighbour's cat was walking on the fence and a strange noise from a car startled them. If the dog down the road then barks at them on our morning walk, they might retaliate in an exaggerated way that does not match the provocation. Because teenage dogs are easily startled and sometimes scared, they will experience more cases of trigger stacking. Some young dogs are over-aroused or stressed all the time, which affects their sleep. In my experience, teenage dogs seem to wake up more during the night than older dogs. The combination of lack of sleep, high activity levels during the day and their developing brain not making correct assessments of situations can create the perfect recipe for disaster: a teenage dog that barks and lunges at minor things.

If we feel that our dog lashes out seemingly for no reason, it might be a good idea to slow and calm things down. They might be overwhelmed and have reached a breaking point. Following a strict routine for a while (at least a couple of weeks) to minimise surprises and making sure our dog gets enough sleep will help them better cope. Keeping a routine means sticking to a regular schedule when they get up, go for walks, train and go to bed. It also means doing the same walks for a while and only venturing farther afield when they are calm. We still keep socialising, but make sure they can cope with the areas we are going to and maybe stick a bit closer to home before we add in novel environments.

8.1.3 Behaviour chains

Isn't it frustrating when we try to train our dog not to jump up, but it gets worse? This may be a part of the *behaviour chain syndrome*, where sequential behaviours are associated with one another through learnt cues. This means that sometimes we end up accidentally training undesirable behavioural associations when dealing with unwanted behaviours. A classic example for this is seen in the pattern when a dog jumps up. Our dog jumps up, we ask for a *sit*, our dog sits and gets a reinforcer. Our dog learns to jump up, then sit and get a reinforcer. That kind of approach will not decrease the jumping but most likely will make it worse. We are unintentionally teaching a behaviour chain – jump–*sit*–treat – that means the dog will not learn to *sit* without jumping. Behaviour chains are not always bad – we can use them to our advantage if we are aware of them and careful about what we reinforce while training (see Section 9.5).

The solution is to teach the behaviour we want first, *sit-stay*, by using a lure and then proofing it. *Proofing* means practicing *sit-stay* in different environments while reinforcing generously; this makes sure our dog 'understands' the cue *sit-stay* in a lot of different contexts and situations. We then must manage carefully and set the dog up for success. If our dog approaches, we ask for *sit-stay* before they can jump on us. It is best to practice this when our dog is not too excited first, for example in our normal training sessions. Once that works, we can practice in more problematic contexts like when a family member comes home.

8.2 How to keep everyone sane

Teenage dogs need much more mental and physical exercise than puppies, because their brain is wired for exploration and they are physically in their prime – with energy to spare! Sometimes it is difficult to find a balance in providing adequate stimulation in both mental and physical realms. Aware of the need for physical stimulation, most humans will take their dogs out for regular walks at least once a day. Walking is still one of the main activities we do with our dogs and can be a great way to bond, spend quality time together and explore the world together.

Walks are great at addressing physical stimulation, but they do not adequately address dogs' need for mental exercise; dogs need a combination of aerobic exercise and brain work to be content. Brain work comes in many forms; for example, fun games, food puzzles and 'sniffaris' (walks where they can sniff at their leisure) keep our dog engaged. If our dog goes out daily for about an hour at least once (for a run or another physical activity) and yet they are not able to calmly relax on their bed, bark at random things, destroy the house or yard or try to get our attention incessantly, the problem might be a lack of mental stimulation. A good indication that we are getting it right is when our teenage dogs can relax, spend time on their own and are able to watch the world go by without getting over-excited.

8.2.1 Enrichment and stimulation

Enrichment – providing rewarding and stimulating challenges, choice and variety that promotes mental and physical health by making the environment more meaningful and valuable – is one way to provide mental stimulation for our dogs. Garvey and colleagues (Purdue University) talk about five types of enrichment that can be used to enhance an animal's quality of life: social (contact with others), occupational (giving them a job, e.g. a dog sport), sensory (sights, music, scents), nutritional (feeding enrichment such as foraging) and physical (e.g. toys or physical features such as platforms)[73]. Research on shelter dogs indicates that even minimal enrichment (two daily training sessions and a food dispensing toy once a day) has a positive effect on their desirable behaviours such as sitting, lying down and being *quiet*[74]. Food enrichment toys for kennelled dogs increases activity levels and lowers barking[75]. Part of enrichment is variety that allows for our dog to make choices when it comes to their daily activities, their food and their social life.

Social Enrichment

Enriching our dogs socially means play, friends and other dogs (this can be dog friends or a companion dog in the same household), car trips to visit family and generally keeping them comfortable with living in a human world (see Section 6.1). We choose our destination in accordance with what we enjoy, too. If we enjoy the coffee shop, we take them there; if we enjoy bushwalks, we do that; if we heard about a new river walk we want to do, we go there. The main goal is to make sure it is fun for all involved.

Social enrichment is required all throughout our dog's life and will help them feel more comfortable with strange people, environments and situations. Taking our teenage dogs to new and different places on a regular basis is important (see Section 6.3) because while dogs enjoy routine, it is important to make sure they do not just *cope* with going to a new place, but actually *enjoy* exploring it. Giving them the confidence to interact with a variety of dogs, humans and environments will allow them to better enjoy novel interactions.

Occupational Enrichment

Occupational enrichment essentially means we need to give our dog a job – lest they invent one for themselves. A job for a teenage dog is learning basic obedience or tricks, engaging in foraging games in the garden, going for walks, spending time at the park, participating in a dog sport (such as agility, obedience, tracking, search-and-rescue, nose work), creating an obstacle course for them in the backyard or becoming a therapy dog (e.g. for retirement homes or hospitals, or less formally, visiting our elderly family members). There are endless job opportunities for dogs and ways of enriching their day-to-day lives, but we humans need to provide them (e.g. training, games and other brain activities).

Shellbe is a dog with a job! We both love agility and you can see how happy and excited she is: her tail is up and she is 'smiling' and focused. This is at a competition and she loves competing, probably because she spends a lot of time with me and her friends. She also gets a lot of treats! Picture Le Hammer.

Sensory Enrichment

Enrichment also means giving our dogs places to hide, dig or sunbath in the yard or even providing them with a sensory garden. A sensory garden provides paths, plants to sniff, as well as areas to hide, rest, explore and linger in during the day[76]. Similarly, providing blankets to let them crawl up under or scented cloths or toys will engage our dog's senses and minds.

While our teenage dogs need to learn to walk on a leash, walks should not just be an exercise in *heeling* but rather a pleasant activity that caters to the human's *and* the dog's needs. Dogs should be allowed to sniff and explore within the range of the leash. I recommend we take our dogs on 'sniffari'[77] walks daily, instead of a boring leash walk. A *sniffari* means we leave the house without a set route but let our dog decide where we go (if it is safe), sniffing to their heart's content (this also addresses the need to provide choice for our dog; see Section 3.2.4). Sometimes we might not go very far because the scents are so interesting that they spend a lot of time sniffing just one small area. Other times we might go further. Often, we will find ourselves exploring places we hadn't even considered to be interesting, and we can start to 'see' the world through our dog's nose.

Sniffing is probably one of the most enjoyable activities for our dogs, especially since smell is their strongest sense (comparable to how humans rely on vision). This leads to a relatively unknown application of animal science in dog training: 'Panksepp's 7 Basic Emotions'[78] (see Section 4.2). One of these basic emotions is the seeking system, which is at the root of many behaviours. In dogs, the seeking system is activated when they do what they are born for, like smelling, herding, chasing, running, eating or socialising. When we are doing something we enjoy, we experience pleasure from the activity itself. This pleasure is caused by the release of dopamine. This means when we let our dogs sniff, their seeking system is activated and they will enjoy the activity, feel pleasure and it will make them mentally tired in an enjoyable way. This can also be thought of in human terms. Smelling is equivalent to reading the 'doggie newspaper' – akin to us checking social media. Our dogs are able to catch up on who was where in the neighbourhood, newcomers, what the cat or the possum did on the fence or where their dog friends met.

Nutritional Enrichment

One form of enrichment for our teenage dogs is using their daily food to keep them entertained, instead of simply feeding them out of a bowl. I compare feeding out of a food bowl to someone putting money into my bank account without me doing anything for it. If someone puts $1000 into my bank account every morning, I probably will not go to work (as much as I love dogs!); I will instead spend the day 'lazing around', getting bored very quickly and inventing jobs for myself like annoying my husband. That is what happens to a lot of teenage dogs. They get a full food bowl every morning, and then they are bored for the rest of the day. Although they shouldn't 'work' for *all* their food, but they also shouldn't *only* eat out of food bowls. I recommend using part of their daily ratio in food-dispensing toys such as Kongs, puzzles or paper rolls (see below) scattered in the yard like a treasure hunt.

Most dogs will prefer foraging for their food and find it more enriching than just eating out of a food bowl. There is even a technical term for this: *contrafreeloading*. This means that even if food is freely available, animals will prefer the food that requires an effort to get[79]. The reason for this seems to be that dogs produce dopamine (a feel-good hormone) when the *opportunity* to gain food appears, not when they *actually* get the food. This is probably like us: looking forward to something is often more enjoyable than actually doing it.

Another form of nutritional enrichment is dietary diversity. I love giving my dogs a variety of different foods. While there are some foods dog should not have (e.g. garlic, onions, chocolate, some nuts), there are a lot of vegetables they can have such as carrots, zucchini, broccoli, peas or celery. Cooked pumpkin and sweet potato can be used in Kongs. I firmly believe dogs get pleasure from different tastes as much as we do and the notion that they need to be fed dry food so every single meal is 'balanced' is nothing more than a marketing spiel. Yes, we should feed a balanced diet, but balance can and should come over time. Would you opt to eat monotonous yet nutritionally-balanced food pellets?

Physical Enrichment

Like humans, dogs get bored with the same toys. It has been proven that dogs like new things, but also that their interest is transient[80]! This is something we dog-humans know already: we get our dog an expensive new toy for Christmas and they either destroy it within minutes or get bored with it just as quickly. This can be expensive. Rotating toys – meaning putting some of them away for a while and then bringing them out again once they've had a chance to be forgotten – helps keep our dog interested in the same toys for longer. Alternatively, we can add a new scent to an old toy (roll them in grass or leaves) or we change the way we play with them (e.g. instead of throwing the toy we might hide it or play tug with it).

 In real life Until Chillax, all my dogs were obsessed with balls. They would chase them all day, every day if I let them and they would train for long periods of time just for their ball. Chillax is different. He loves new things and this goes for toys and food. He gets bored very quickly with the same-old, same-old. He will chase a ball up to five times and then ask: *Ok what's next?* He will train well for cheese for five minutes and then loses interest. From Chillax, I learnt that if we have a dog who loves 'new stuff' we will need to up our training game. With Chillax I now have at least three different types of food with me when I seriously train (e.g. cheese, boiled chicken and some shop-bought treats) and I also have different toys – and some of them are only ever used in a training context.

There are uncountable toys available at the pet shop these days, but enrichment does not need to cost the earth (or your bank account). There are a lot of home-made enrichment toys that are cheap and often our dogs like them even better than the expensive toys from the pet shop. For example, paper rolls can be filled with a few treats and crunched up on both sides so our dog must chew the cardboard to get to the treats.

An empty 600 ml water bottle (lid removed) can be filled with dry food and our dog will spend a fair amount of time trying to get the food out while batting it around. Another option is empty cardboard boxes with a few treats in them. If you want to be fancier just do an internet search for 'homemade enrichment toys for dogs'.

This can also be a fun activity for your children. This will help the children to see things from the dog's perspective – for example can they reach the food with their paw, or is it safe to destroy the plastic bottle? Based on their personalised knowledge of their dogs, the kids will be given the chance to design engaging activities that are individualised and enjoyable with whatever spare materials are lying around the house (and are safe for dogs). Beyond the creativity this brings out in children, it also gets them away from screens and might help them better relate to their family (dogs) and feel empathy for them. The book *Canine Enrichment For the Real World* has some great, creative ideas[81].

8.2.2 Relaxing down-time

In addition to keeping our dog's mind busy, it is important to make sure our dog has appropriate rest and down time with us, inside (see Section 3.2.1). This is even more crucial for teenage dogs who find the outside world a bit scary when they are going through a secondary fear phase. A weekly rest day where we just spend time at home, do some training, play fun games and maybe 'hunt' for food in the backyard can help them relax and calm down. See Chapter 7 on encouraging and promoting calmness in our dog.

8.2.3 Don't ignore – or yell about – the bad, and make sure you look for the good!

I know many well-meaning friends and ill-advised trainers who recommend ignoring the 'bad' things our dog does. They are under the impression that ignoring a behaviour will make it go away. The theory behind it is that because the behaviour does not get any feedback (positive or negative) it will fade away. Technically we call this *extinction*. However, just ignoring bad behaviour without providing guidance on what to do instead can also create a lot of frustration for our dogs (and us) because it takes a long time for a behaviour to extinguish. There is also a phenomenon called *extinction burst*, which means that if you try to get rid of a behaviour by ignoring it, it will get worse before it gets better. For example, imagine this situation: our dogs barks at us when we have dinner because they want some food from the table, which we previously provided. If we now stop giving them food without providing an alternative behaviour which we reinforce (like *go-to-mat*), they will try extra hard to ask for the food – after all, it has worked so far.

But, ignoring 'bad' behaviour is not a good idea for other reasons, too. For example, we cannot ignore our teenage dogs when they jump on visitors because some visitors are afraid of dogs, it can hurt when they jump and (as mentioned earlier) they are practicing the wrong thing and becoming more proficient at it. We also cannot ignore when they bark at everything that moves or take it upon themselves to empty the rubbish bin (unless we consider the bin an enrichment toy – just joking!).

It is tempting, when we see bad behaviour, to scream *no!* However, it is almost impossible to teach dogs or humans what *not* to do. Screaming *no!* is not the best way to deal with our teenage dogs unwanted behaviours; it can lead to reinforcing the wrong behaviour because a lot of the unwanted behaviours are driven by the need for attention. If we scream *no* that still gives our dog attention – which is what they wanted in the first place. Additionally, we too often get stuck in the 'don't jump up', 'don't go onto the couch', 'don't bark', 'don't, don't, don't'. 'Don't' or 'no' is a *concept* and not a *behaviour*! While we can use 'concept training' for dogs as mentioned earlier (see Section 3.1.1), 'no' is probably not the easiest to teach. Dogs have a hard time understanding this. I am not saying a harsh *no* cannot stop a behaviour – but the dog does not have any more information on what we want them *to* do, or what the problem was in the first place. This is the situation described earlier (see Section 3.2.3) when relaxing on a bed and someone starts yelling at us in a foreign language. They clearly don't want us to lie there, but what are we supposed to do instead? What can we do that won't result in being hit? And how unfair is this?

> **Training tip** Rather than saying 'no', if we need to stop our dog from doing something it is better to use: *interrupt* (with their name), *redirect* (ask for another behaviour) and *reinforce* (with a treat, toy, chew, etc.) (see Section 9.3). If our dog barks at a visitor, *interrupt* them by calling their name, *redirect* them to go to bed and *reinforce* them being on the bed. We need to make sure that there are about five seconds between the unwanted behaviour (barking), the new behaviour (being on the bed) and the reinforcer (a chew) because we do not want to reinforce the barking by mistake (see Section 8.1.3). We also should have taught the new behaviour before we are using it in a difficult situation for our dogs.

It also pays to look for the good things and reinforce these instead of concentrating too much on the unwanted behaviours (see Section 7.3). I love the idea of 50 treats a day. This is an idea from Sdao in her book *Plenty In Life Is Free*. If you have not read her book, check it out – it is a great read[82].

First, we make a list of ten things we want our dog to do more often; for example, relax on the bed, sit-for-greeting, approach calmly, etc. We then count out 50 treats or pieces of normal food-kibble in the morning and have them somewhere handy so we can quickly access them when needed. Every time our dog does something that is on our list, we give them a treat. This has two advantages: we focus on the good things because we need to use 50 treats and the dog does more of the good things because they get reinforced more often. It also helps us humans to stop and appreciate how much our dogs do right, rather than focusing on the negatives (a key step in retraining ourselves; see Section 5.3).

8.3 Summary

Trying to keep our own and our teenage dog's sanity can be a challenge. They need to learn social etiquette despite their startle responses and trigger stacking. We must also be aware of unintentionally teaching behaviour chains. However, with appropriate and creative enrichment and stimulation at home, providing jobs, leisurely sniffaris and special social outings we should be able to keep it together and have some fun, even during the challenging teenage phase! When dealing with 'bad' behaviours it is important to realise that these are normal dog behaviours, but we shouldn't yell about, or ignore, them – instead we should teach them an alternative, acceptable behaviour. At the same time, we should look for and reward the good.

Chapter 9
How to?

Ok, so we've gotten this far in understanding our dogs' needs, we have acknowledged the importance of relationships, communication, animal emotions, positive reinforcement, socialisation and training, teaching and recognising calm and keeping everyone sane. But what does this training actually look like? What is it premised on? This section will first explain operant and respondent conditioning, in which context they are used, then provide step-by-step guidance on how to teach the basics and more complex behaviours while applying these forms of conditioning.

9.1 Operant and respondent conditioning

When teaching and educating dogs we use two distinct approaches. If we teach so-called 'obedience' behaviours such as *sit*, *heel* and loose leash walking, etc. we are using *operant conditioning*. However, there is another form of conditioning called *classical* or *respondent conditioning*, which is trying to change our dog's perception of a stimulus and condition a positive emotional response. While it makes sense to describe these two approaches separately, we have to be aware that they often (if not always) happen at the same time.

9.1.1 Operant conditioning; Markers and reinforcers

Operant conditioning (see Section 5.1 for a definition) means we are teaching our dog a behaviour and reinforcing it if they respond correctly (e.g. *sit* or *lie-down*). Using positive reinforcement in training means we add something our dogs want when they do the right thing (see Section 5.1). The thing we add is technically called a *reinforcer* and it depends on us, our dog and the situation. We often use food because most dogs like food and it can be delivered quickly. We can also use play, a toy, pats or praise. Just keep in mind that in the early days, food is your (and your dog's) best friend and will most likely gets you better results than any other reinforcer.

It is helpful to use a *marker* when using operant conditioning. A marker is also called a *bridge* because it bridges the time between the behaviour and the reinforcer. A marker is a sound – a short word like *yes* or *good*, or a clicker, and lets our dog know that they have done the right thing and a reinforcer (treat, ball, toy, pat) is on its way. To teach our dog what the marker means we say *yes* (or click) and deliver a reinforcer. We will only need a few repetitions! Our dogs figure that one out very quickly. We call this sequence '*mark* and *reinforce*'.

We should mark as soon as our dog offers the behaviour we want because the marker serves as a bridge between the behaviour and the reinforcer – it *promises* a reinforcer but does not *replace* the reinforcer. By bridging the time from the behaviour to the reinforcer, it helps our dog more accurately pinpoint the exact action that will get them the reinforcer. This is because the marker is much faster feedback and more clearly indicates to them that their immediate, precise behaviour is what will get them the reinforcer (not whatever behaviour they are doing by the time the treat or pat arrives, which will be delayed by several seconds). Timing is important. For example, if we ask for a *sit*, we mark as soon as their rear end hits the ground, then follow calmly with a reinforcer. If we do not mark, they might make the wrong association for which behaviour gets them the reinforcer. In Horowitz's[83] words, marking 'helps make a human moment salient to a dog; left to his own devices, the dog parcels up his life differently.'

There are different ways of teaching our teenage dogs using operant conditioning. The three main approaches we use are luring, shaping and capturing (see Section 5.2). *Luring* means we guide the dog into the position we are asking for with a treat in our hand. Once the dog is in the correct position we *mark* and *reinforce*. *Shaping* means we use a marker to communicate to our dog that they are on the right track. Shaping is 'the differential reinforcement of successive approximations toward a target behavior'[84]. While that sounds impressive it just means reinforcing small steps towards the end, desirable behaviour, until we reach our goal. *Capturing* means we wait until our dog does something we like (e.g. being on their bed) and we then reinforce this behaviour.

> **Training tip** Check out Goodogs's YouTube channel for videos on how we use luring and shaping[85]. For luring, *Puppy's First Day At Home*[86] is a good one. There is also a video called *Close The Door*[87] that shows how shaping is done.

When teaching our teenage dog the basics, we mostly use **luring** and we need to make sure we are using it effectively. When we lure, we show the food (if that's what we are using as a reinforcer, but we can also use a toy) and guide them into the position. However, as soon as our dog understands what we want, we need to take the reinforcer out of the luring hand and have it either in a treat pouch or in the other hand behind our back. For most behaviours, luring (meaning the food is in the hand and visible to our dog) should only be necessary for three to four repetitions and after that it should become a hand cue. We want them to do the behaviour without seeing the lure. If we do not phase out the lure, they will only do it when the see the food or toy – this is bribing. This does not mean we do not reinforce! It just means they do the behaviour when we cue and *then* (after marking), we give them the toy or food. This way they learn to respond to the cue without being bribed with visible food.

> 🦴 **Training tip** One of the main complaints we have in our
> classes is that teenage dogs only do the requested behaviour
> when they see the food reward. This means we have lured for too
> long and our dog becomes dependent on seeing the food and will not
> do what we ask if they cannot see the food. The food then becomes a
> bribe and the dog has not learnt the cue but just follows the treat.
> Switching from luring to a cue is important and should happen after
> a few repetitions. Another thing my clients ask is 'shouldn't my dog
> do it because I said so or because they love me?' I don't know about
> you, but I do not work for free (almost no one does!). I am sure our
> dogs love us, but that is not a reinforcer for specific behaviours and
> certainly not enough for training. Performance correlates with the
> quality and the quantity of the treats we are using as reinforcers.
> Food – and especially good food – is their currency.

When luring, the lure motion becomes the initial visual cue, looking as if we still had food in the hand. We then gradually change it to a more abstract gesture like a flat hand raised above their head for a *sit* or flat hand lowered in front of them for a *lie-down*. The final hand signal is always an 'abstract' form of the lure motion.

The easiest example is a *sit*: When our dog is standing facing us, we hold the food in front of our dog's nose (palm facing up) and move it up and over their head. They will follow the food with their head and their rear end naturally goes down into a *sit*; thus, we are guiding their body into the correct position by manipulating their movement. As soon as their rear end hits the floor, we *mark* and *reinforce*. We then repeat another two to three times with the food in our hand. For the next repetition we act like the food is still in our hand but then reinforce from our other hand. We then gradually change to a flat hand and it eventually it becomes a symbolic hand signal; reinforcements come from the other hand.

Good practice is to put the verbal cue to the behaviour only once it is well-established for our dog. This means that if they, for example, *sit* at a rate of about 80% when they see the hand signal, we then put the verbal cue to it. The reason we do not say the verbal cue earlier is that they might make the wrong association. If we say *sit* when they are still standing, they might think that is *sit*. Or, if we say it when they are halfway down, they might think that is *sit*. Therefore, it is important for them to already have an association between a visual cue and the appropriate behaviour before introducing a verbal cue. When we want to introduce a verbal cue, it is important to say *sit* first, then give the hand signal, then *mark* and *reinforce* when they *sit*. If we do it the other way around the hand signal will overshadow the word, meaning they will probably not even hear it but just stick with what they know (the hand signal). The exceptions to this 'rule' to teach a hand signal first and a verbal cue second are *drop-it* or *come*. I think it is beneficial to have a hand signal and verbal cue for most behaviours, especially since there are times when they cannot see us and times they cannot hear us so having a multimodal system of communication is helpful.

 In real life Dogs will learn to work for longer periods of times without reinforcers and can learn to delay gratifications – but this only works if we deliver reinforcers at some point. For example, my dogs and I compete in Rally Obedience and Agility. When we win, we are not winning because my dogs love me (I am sure they do) but because they know there is barbeque chicken, smoked salmon and organic beef patties at the end. They know this because we train a lot and they have learnt there is something amazing in it for them.

9.1.2 Respondent conditioning

The definition of respondent (or classical) conditioning is 'a process that involves creating an association between a naturally existing stimulus and a previously neutral one'[88]. This may sound confusing, but let's break it down: the classical conditioning process involves pairing a previously neutral stimulus (e.g. the sound of a bell, in Pavlov's infamous experiments with dogs) with an unconditioned stimulus (e.g. the taste of food). This *unconditioned stimulus* (the food in Pavlov's example) naturally and automatically triggers the salivating response and we call this the *unconditioned response*. After associating the neutral stimulus and the unconditioned stimulus, the sound of the bell alone will start to evoke salivating as a response. The sound of the bell is now known as the *conditioned stimulus* and salivating in response to the bell is known as the *conditioned response*.

This approach is used when we try to change our teenage dog's perception of a stimulus. Teenage dogs are prone to perceive novel things as scary because their brains are not processing the information correctly (see Section 2.2) so our teenage dogs may require more work in counter-conditioning than puppies or adult dogs. In our case we are not working with a neutral stimulus but most likely something our dog finds scary. The process we are using is called desensitising and counter-conditioning.

Desensitisation is the gradual exposure to a stimulus that elicits an undesirable response (e.g. lunging or barking at the bicycle), but below the threshold that elicits the response. Desensitisation means we are very gradually exposing our dog to the scary thing by starting at a very low stress level and building up slowly. This essentially means we need to start far away from the stimulus. With time and repetition, our dog becomes less reactive to the stimulus and can tolerate higher intensity (being closer). A desensitising protocol usually involves counter-conditioning as one of the steps[89].

Counter-conditioning means a conditioned stimulus (e.g. a scary bicycle) is paired with an unconditioned stimulus (e.g. food) to undo the effects (e.g. fear) of an earlier association. Every time the scary thing appears, we give our dog a treat, even if they bark or lunge. During this process we try to stay under threshold, meaning our dog does not bark or lunge, but if they do, we still give them a treat anyway because we are trying to condition a positive emotional response (counter-conditioning). If they bark and lunge it means *we* made a mistake by being too close and we need to increase distance. During this conditioning process we are 'paying' for the *presence* of the stimulus, not for 'being good', which is what we do in operant conditioning. We need a plan for this so we can do it systematically. At every step, we need to ensure our dog is happy and comfortable. If our dog gets scared, we need to go back to an easier/lower-stress stage. If we ignore that they are frightened, we will make their fears worse.

As an example of what 'desensitising counter-conditioning' looks like in practice, consider a dog who is scared of a child on a bicycle. We will use desensitising and counter-conditioning to change their perception of the stimulus and create a positive association. Starting with the child and bicycle being at a distance where our dog feels safe and happy, we wait for them to look at the child, and then we *mark* and deliver a treat. We then gradually decrease the distance to the child, closely watching our dog for signs of stress. We will only go as close as our dog is able to remain relaxed. With each glance they make towards the child, we *mark* and *deliver a treat*. With enough repetitions, they will perceive the previously-scary thing as either neutral or positive, because child-on-bicycle now equals a treat.

There is some discussion amongst trainers if we should mark during this process or just deliver a treat when they see the scary 'thing'. I think it does not matter and it works with or without marker. But what is important is that we only deliver the treat once our dog has seen the scary 'thing'. If we give them the treat to distract them before they see it, we will create the opposite effect and will sensitise – meaning our treat will now predict the scary thing.

9.2 Distance – duration – distraction

When training we often refer to the 3Ds, talking about *distance, duration* and *distraction*. What it means is that we should only raise one challenge at a time. For example, when we train a *stay*, we first work in a non-distracting environment like our loungeroom, only asking for a very short *stay* as we stand right in front of our dog. Once they are proficient at this, we then gradually raise one criterion at a time. We are still in the lounge-room and very close to our dog but ask for longer *stay* (i.e. duration). If we are successful, we move a little further away (i.e. distance) and if that works, we go to the backyard where there are birds (i.e. distraction). We keep raising our criteria until we have reached our goal. This could be a 30-minute stay on a mat at our favourite coffee shop!

 In real life I was at the off-leash area and two horses had their head over the fence looking at my dogs. Chillax had met horses before, but not that close. I put him on the leash and let him go as close as he wanted. He stopped about three metres in front of the horses. I fed him treats for a few seconds and we moved on. Next time when we came around, he went a bit closer and I gave him more treats. The third time we came past he ran towards the horses and I expected him to bark, but he went closer than the last couple of times and offered a 'play bow'. With two exposures and positively associating the horses, he had formed a positive association and felt safe enough to interact. Sometimes respondent conditioning gets amazing results very quickly!

9.3 Interrupt – redirect – reinforce

When things go wrong (and sometimes it is an emergency), we cannot just ignore and watch our dog do the wrong thing while they figure it out for themselves. In these situations, we will distract our dog from the unwanted behaviour by calling their name in a neutral tone (interrupt), ask them for a different, incompatible behaviour (redirect) and reward them for doing what we ask (reinforce). For example, our dog barks at the delivery guy who came to the door unexpected: We calmly call their name (interrupt), ask them to go to their bed (redirect) and give them a chew on their bed (reinforce).

9.4 Environmental management

All behaviours – including the inconvenient ones for humans – become stronger when they are repeated. We all know 'practice makes perfect' and 'old habits die hard'. This is especially true for teenage dogs because new pathways in the brain form readily during this time and it also means that if the wrong pathways are established it will be harder to change them later in life. This means we must manipulate the environment in such a way that there are not too many opportunities for our dogs to repeat unacceptable behaviour until we have trained an alternative, acceptable behaviour. Technically speaking, we are changing the *antecedent* – what comes before the behaviour – to prevent our dog from making the same mistake repeatedly. We can also just call it good management. Overall, to be successful we need to manipulate the environment is such a way that our dogs can succeed, meaning teaching in an environment with less distraction and more distance (see Section 9.2).

An example is when people come to the house and we want to prevent our exuberant teenage dog from jumping on them. Management means putting our dog in a different room, using baby gates or leashes to prevent them from jumping on visitors at the door. We do this until we have taught a different, acceptable behaviour like *sit-stay*. In most cases management is not a long-term solution, and does not replace training, but can help the dog get it right (or, at least, prevent them from learning how to do it wrong) until we have taught and reinforced the alternative.

We need to keep in mind that we are not the only ones reinforcing our dogs. The environment does, too and it may end up reinforcing bad behaviour. In this context I call the environment anything but us. This can be another person, dog, birds, a sandwich left on the counter or the postman. All these things (and many more) are highly reinforcing for our dogs and can be much more rewarding than anything we have to offer. Chasing a bird for a hunting dog will most likely trump our offer of food, while barking at intruders (and making them go away) is probably more reinforcing than a game of tug for most dogs. This means if we do not manage the environment carefully, these other reinforcers can be more powerful than what we have to offer and will sabotage our training. Therefore, we also need to manage the environment before we leave for work in the morning, in anticipation of what factors may unintentionally reward certain behaviours while we are out. It helps to close the blinds, turn the radio on, close the windows against noise or leave them in rooms away from the busy street.

 In real life The postman is delivering the mail. Our dog sits behind the window and sees the postman coming. They start barking, the postman delivers the mail and leaves. Our dog barks until the postman disappears. What do you think our dog thinks? They think they did a very good job of scaring away the evil postman and keeping the house safe – every single day. The barking is reinforced and will increase. No one told the dog that this is what postmen do – meanwhile, we get frustrated that this is what dogs do! This means we need to manage the environment in such a way that they do not see the postman until we have counter conditioned the postman and trained a more appropriate behaviour i.e. *go-to-mat*. If done properly this can even work when we are not at home because we have changed their underlying perception with the postman!

Training tip I think I am good trainer, but I cannot train when I am not at home or asleep. This means if I have a barky dog, I will keep them away from the windows where external stimuli will trigger barking and will only let them have access to these problematic areas when they have learnt to be calm.

9.5 Back-chaining and behaviour chains

A *behaviour chain* is a learnt (cued) association of a sequence of behaviours and we can use it to our advantage when teaching more complex behaviours. For example, *go-to-mat* is a useful behaviour chain that consist of three behaviours: *go-to-mat*, *lie-down* on the mat and *stay* there. In this case we are training a behaviour chain (on purpose) by using *back-chaining*. This simply means we teach the last behaviour first and make each step very rewarding. The last behaviour then becomes a reinforcer for the one that precedes it, as our dog learns to associate one behaviour with another (and reinforcers!). If we teach the *go-to-mat* sequence, *stay* on the mat (which has been reinforced with a treat of some kind) becomes the reinforcer for *lie-down*, which reinforces the *go-to-mat* cue (see Section 9.8.1 for how to train each step).

Behaviour chains may work against us if we find we are unintentionally reinforcing an undesirable behaviour (see Section 8.1.3). There is nothing wrong with behaviour chains but we need to make sure we are teaching the right ones. If we are trying to solve a problem and it gets worse, we are probably teaching a behaviour chain by mistake.

9.6 Beyond food treats: Life rewards and Premack

While food is great in training, we should mix it up with praise, toys, social interaction and other life rewards. A life reward is anything our dog wants and enjoys in daily life. This requires we know our dog's individual preferences. This can be access to something they want (e.g. a person or another dog), an activity such as a game, being able to chase that bird or a splash in the river. An example for a life reward is giving our dog access to the yard when they ask. Let's assume our dog is calmly standing near the door to the yard and wants to go out for a play and a sniff. They look at us, not scratching the door. Reinforce this by opening the door and letting them play and sniff around. Or say we are arriving at the dog park, still on the leash. We ask our dog for a *sit* and the reinforcer/life reward is that they can go off-leash. Or perhaps we are on a walk and our dog calmly walks past a barking dog. We can then start running and have a play. This gets us away from the barking dog and is a reinforcer for our dog. No need for food or toys, just an understanding of communication and preferences!

Another concept is the Premack principle; it is the 'eat your veggies and you get the ice cream' approach in dog-training. More scientifically, this is using a more-probable behaviour to reinforce a less-probable behaviour. The likelihood of our dog chasing a possum is higher than maintaining a *sit* when they see the possum. The chase is a more-probable than *sit* (and more rewarding). The way to deal with this is to ask for a *sit* (make sure we are either behind a fence or the possum is in a tree so no possum gets hurt) when they see the possum and after they *sit* we release them by saying *ok*, and let them chase the out-of-reach possum. Thus, our dogs are being rewarded for 'eating their veggies' (sitting, a less-probable behaviour) by 'getting the ice cream' (chasing, a more-probable behaviour).

 In real life I was at an agility training session and there were birds on the field. Shellbe did a great agility run despite seeing the birds. Once she crossed the finishing line, I let her chase the birds instead of giving her treats. She did and once they were gone, she happily came back all smiles. A friend asked: *Shouldn't you prevent her from chasing the birds?* Her fear was that she would chase birds indiscriminately. However, Shellbe and I have a close understanding and she only chases bird when I give her permission. I know that she loves chasing them, so I use it as a reinforcer when possible. Using what our dog really wants as a reinforcer will work in our favour.

9.7 The basics

In the following sections I will introduce the basic cues every teenage dog should have in their toolbox: *watch-me, hand-touch,* Doggy-Zen, *sit-stay, lie-down, leave-it, quiet* and *come.* I call the first three 'control behaviours' – all of them bring attention back to us so that our dog focuses on us and what we ask them to do (instead of trying to play with other dogs, jump on people or chase the cat on the fence). *Watch-me* brings our teenage dogs' attention back to us and establishes a line of communication. If they have not learnt to look at us and pay attention to what we are saying, they will have a hard time following any other cues. The *hand-touch* cue has the same function of bringing attention back to us but is easier to use when we walk with our dogs as they can touch our hand and keep moving at the same time. This is sometimes more helpful than the *watch-me* cue because we increase distance and move away from the distraction all at the same time. The *hand-touch* can also be used when we teach loose-leash walking by getting our dog to touch our hand while they walk next to us. Doggy-Zen is a calming exercise to reduce stress levels when worked up.

Sit-stay or *lie-down* are foundation behaviours we use when we need to redirect our dogs from other unwanted behaviour (such as jumping up), or when we ask them to *go-to-their-mat* or the start of crate training. *Leave-it* and *drop-it* is used to prevent them from picking up the dead rat or possum or any other rubbish on a walk. *Quiet* is an essential cue for any dog in our densely-populate suburban area because a lot of times we want them to stop barking despite the 'intruders' on the doorstep or the barking dog down the street. *Come* is necessary to keep our dog safe, within reach and sometimes getting them out of trouble. It is also a legal requirement – called 'effective control' – to be able to call our dogs back to us when necessary.

9.7.1 Watch-me

This can be done with our dog either sitting or standing in front of us. We ask for *watch-me* by bringing the treat past the dog's nose and up to our eyes, pointing at our eyes – this then becomes the hand cue for *watch-me*. As soon as our dog gives eye contact, we *mark* and *reinforce*. We then gradually ask for longer eye contact. I aim for about ten seconds of steady eye contact. Once the behaviour is established, we then add the verbal cue *watch-me*.

9.7.2 Hand-touch

We start by presenting our flat hand (no treat) about ten centimetres to the right or left of our dog's nose. Normally our dog will touch our hand with their nose, out of curiosity. As soon as they do so, we *mark* and *reinforce* (with treats in our other hand). We should not hold our hand right in front of their nose, as they often find that scary and will not touch it. We also do not want our dog to learn that we will bridge the distance between our hand and their nose – they must actively move their nose towards our hand. If they don't do it, we take our hand away and re-present it on the other side. The hand cue is a flat hand which can be positioned anywhere where the dog can reach it (some dogs love to jump and touch the flat hand!). Once established we can add a verbal cue *hand-touch* but often the hand is enough of a cue to get them to touch it.

9.7.3 Doggy-Zen

This is not a cued behaviour, but rather a relaxation exercise. Like us, our teenage dogs need to learn to de-stress and calm their mind (see Chapter 7). Anyone who has done yoga or meditation knows that calming the mind is not easy and dogs are no different. Once they are stressed or just excited it is difficult to calm down. I have found Doggy-Zen to be a good way of slowing things down for our dogs.

For the Doggy-Zen exercise, we show our calm dog the treat (in our hand) and then extend our arm out fully to the right of our head (at eye level). We then wait until our dog takes their eyes off the treat and gives us eye contact. We must not say anything. Once we get eye contact, we *mark* and *reinforce*. In the beginning we *mark* and *reinforce* for every glance! But as our dogs improve, we wait longer and will reinforce only for extended eye contact. We aim for five to ten seconds.

Because this exercise is not cued our dog needs to figure out what gets them the treat. An excited dog has a hard time taking their eyes off the treat because the shortest way to the treat is looking at the hand with the treat. However, in this case, that is not working. To get the treat they need to take their eyes off the treat and look at us. When they are excited their brain is not processing information properly and they have poor impulse control which makes it difficult for them to figure it out. A typical teenage problem! But, once they calm down, they are able to take their eyes off the treat and look at us. We can literally watch them relax and often, they will take a deep breath, too.

We should practice this 'meditation' initially when they are calm, as this will help create a pathway in the brain that promotes relaxation. Once our dog understands this exercise, we can start practicing in more exciting environments. Because we have practiced this relaxation exercise and have create new pathways in the brain, they can now do it even when they are excited.

9.7.4 Sit-stay

Sit is taught by having a treat in our hand, palm facing up and bringing the treat over and towards the back of our dog's head. As they follow the treat, their rear end goes down and they sit. We *mark* and *reinforce*. In the very beginning we say *sit* once their rear end touches the floor, but over time they will learn what *sit* means – it becomes a verbal cue – and when we say *sit* they will sit down.

After mastering *sit*, we can move on to *sit-stay*. To teach the *sit-stay* cue we give the verbal or hand-signal *sit* cue. We then withhold the treat for a second or two to keep them seated (*sit-stay*). *Sit* should be a stationary behaviour – it is not rear end on the floor and then straight up again. We can then add a *stay* cue. This can be either a verbal *stay* or a hand-signal (open hand facing towards them, like you're telling someone to stop). By delaying the marker and reinforcer we gradually teach them to stay seated for longer periods of time.

9.7.5 *Lie-down*

Lie-down is best taught from a sitting position. The dog sits and we guide them with a treat in our hand (palm facing down because the hand signal will be our hand moving towards the ground) slowly into a lying position. Once their chest touches the floor we *mark* and *reinforce*. If our dog stands up, we have moved the treat too far away from them or moved our hand too quickly. Ask for a *sit* and try again, keeping the treat closer to their mouth, moving slowly.

9.7.6 *Leave-it* and *drop-it*

We should teach the *leave-it* cue to prevent our dogs from picking up BBQ skewers, cooked chicken bones, McDonald wrappers or any other rubbish that is lying around in the streets they shouldn't have when we are out walking. We start by first teaching a *head-turn*, by luring our dog to turn their head to the right or left, holding the treat between our thumb and the middle finger, the index finger straight. The straight index finger moving to the right or left becomes the hand signal for *head-turn* and, eventually, *leave-it*. Once they understand the cue and turn their head, we present a toy and ask them to turn their head away from it and *mark* and *reinforce*. Once that works, we can present food in our hand and ask for *leave-it*, meaning they turn their head away from the food. Once we get a reliable *head-turn* away from the toy and food, we can put the toy or food on the floor and ask for *leave-it* and then *mark* and *reinforce*. If we are training it is good practice to let our dog have the toy/food when we have finished the training session. This way they learn that giving up a prized possession is only temporary and they often can have it once we have checked that is ok for them to have.

Sometimes, our dog obviously cannot have what they've grabbed because it is dangerous or we really don't want them to chew something that is (in our opinion) disgusting. If they already have the dead rat or cigarette pack in their mouth, we should use a *drop-it* cue. *Drop-it* is for stuff they have already in their mouth, *leave-it* for things they are about to grab. *Drop-it* means drop whatever you have in your mouth immediately. We teach this by offering them something more valuable (or tasty) than what they have. To train this, we start by letting them have a toy that they are a little bit interested in but are happy to give up for a treat. They have the toy in their mouth, we show them the treat and as soon as they open their mouth we *mark* and *reinforce*. Once they drop the toy reliably, we add the cue *drop-it*. The next step is a more interesting toy, then their favourite toy and then a chew. In this case, we are not really luring (guiding them into a position following the treat), which means we do not have a visual cue but only a verbal one.

9.7.7 Quiet

When our dog is calm and quiet, we show them a treat, put a finger in front of our lips (think: the classic 'shush' gesture) say *quiet* and give them the treat. We are teaching them that *quiet* will get them a treat.

We then do the same when they bark or are otherwise not being calm: show them the treat, say *quiet* and once they are *quiet*, we give them the treat. We have to make sure that there is at least five seconds between the barking and the treat, otherwise we might reward the barking by mistake (see Section 8.1.3).

9.7.8 *Come*: How to train a great recall

Of all the basic cues to teach our dog, *come* is probably the most important and sometimes the most difficult. In any situation, *come* has many benefits and can avoid real problems for both us and our dogs, such as: being hit by a car, having a confrontation with another dog, meeting a snake or encountering a child that fears dogs. It means that we have effective control over our dog. Unfortunately, though, for some dogs *come* means 'run as far away as you possibly can' (if possible, migrate to the next country, or at least the next dog park). These dogs have learnt that *come* means 'we are going home and the fun is over'. Dogs do not come back because there is a whole-wide world out there that is very rewarding, and off-leash time is often the best part of their day! However, *come* should not mean the *end* of the fun – it should be the *start* of something exciting and fun! For example, playing a game of tug-of-war or the food toss game when they return to us can make all the difference.

> **Training tip** The food toss game goes like this: We throw a small piece of food (it needs to be visible; cheese works well) about a metre to the right of us. The dog runs to the treat and eats it, then looks to us for more. As soon as they look at us, we *mark* and throw the next piece of food. They eat, look at us, throw the next piece. Start with six to seven repetitions. Once our dog understands the game, we throw the treats further and the game becomes more animated. The last piece is fed from the hand – that way they are close enough so we can touch their collar and, if necessary, hold onto them.

For *come,* use the verbal cue (*come;* see below) and then add in the visual, hand cue (outstretched arms over our head). I introduce the verbal cue first because when we teach what *come* means (as described below) it is easier to say the word *come* when they move towards us than trying to get them to follow us with outstretched arms over our head. This visual cue is used because it is recognisable from far away, but it makes training in close proximity a bit more difficult, which is why we start with the verbal cue.

A key point to remember is that if our dog does not respond to our cue to *come,* we should not just keep calling them, as our voice will just become 'white noise' to them. And we shouldn't take it personally if they don't come back – the environment is a great attraction for teenage dogs! It is all part of the learning process. Fortunately, it is possible and very rewarding to teach our dog to *come* if we stick to some basic rules, which are expanded on below:

- Teach our dog what *come* means
- Make it worthwhile for our dog
- Manage the environment and prevent self-reinforcing patterns
- If we are in the dog park, we let them go again
- Never, *ever* punish or rouse on a dog who has come back

Teach our dog what come means

We start by holding a reinforcer (piece of food or a toy) in our hand, showing it to our dog and moving backwards. When our dog moves towards us, we say *come.* As soon as our dog catches up, we give them the reinforcer. We are associating the word *come* with moving towards us. Once they are close enough, we gently touch their collar. This is a safety measure so we can get our hands on our dog in an emergency and helps to prevent creating a 'drive by dog' (a dog who comes, takes the treat and takes off again). Once the dog understands this, we introduce some simple distractions (see Section 9.2). For example, we may call our dog so they have to weave between family members in the house or the backyard. This makes it a great game. We then take this game to a slightly more distracting environment like a fenced dog park at low traffic times. At that stage we can add the visual cue of outstretched arms over our head. This cue is important if they cannot hear but might still be able to see us.

Make it worthwhile for our dog

We must figure out what is most rewarding for our dog and this may be highly individualised. Is it a specific squeaky toy, a chance to play with us, a cuddle or some nice treat (e.g. with the food toss game)? It may even be a more creative 'life reward' (see Section 9.6). Once we have figured this out, we can use this special reinforcer for *come*. We should not ever phase out the reinforcer and we cannot be stingy; a pat on the head will not cut it. A generous reinforcer improves motivation and ultimately their (and our) success.

> **Training tip** One way to make it worthwhile for our dog to *come* is through jackpots. A jackpot is an unexpected, high-value reinforcer. For example, we may give ten treats (one after the other) instead of just one. Or, we may use a favourite tug toy our dog has not seen for a while and have a longer-than-usual play session. It is a bit like people on pokie machines – and we know how well that works at encouraging further gambling! Overall, a jackpot increases motivation and makes both us humans and our dogs feel good.

Manage the environment and prevent self-reinforcing patterns

In the early stages we will have to manage the environment very carefully and keep our dog on a long leash or in fenced areas (see Section 9.4). We can then gradually make it more difficult by going to a fenced area with only a few dogs. We then can try when it is a little bit busier. Keep in mind, the environment can be more reinforcing than what we have to offer! This means we need to work first in environments where what we have (treats, toys, play etc) is the best thing available. If, for example, we cannot prevent access to other dogs with a long leash and our dog finds other dogs reinforcing, they will approach the other dogs rather than us. This means they now have self-reinforced not coming and will most likely repeat that behaviour. So, start with as few distractions as possible to prevent undesirable self-reinforcing patterns.

If we are in the dog park, let them go again

If we are in the dog park, we should call our dog every four to maybe ten minutes with a happy voice, give them a nice treat or have a quick play and then let them go again. This teaches them that *come* does not mean the end of the fun. We should also reinforce when they are checking in with us. This means when they approach voluntary, we give them a treat.

However, there is obviously a time when we do actually need to go home. Once the recall is well-trained, we can just call our dog, give them a tasty treat, clip the leash on and go. However, in the early days we should go and get them so they do not associate *come* with going home.

Never, ever punish or rouse on a dog who comes

Even if it takes us two hours to get our dog to *come*, we must reward them for eventually coming back. If we punish our dog, this positive punishment (see Section 5.1) will only set back our training efforts by teaching them that *come* will earn them a reprimand. Our dog is just showing us that we need to improve our training!

9.8 Advanced training

This section introduces some useful behaviours that might take a little bit more training but are well worth the effort. *Go-to-mat* and/or crate training are prerequisites for harmoniously living together. Walking on the leash and *meet-and-greet* skills are essential to make outings a pleasant experience for both humans and dogs. Tricks improve the relationship and are fun. Husbandry behaviours help with the daily care for our teenage dog and vet visits, making these necessary events less stressful for us and our dog.

9.8.1 *Go-to-mat, stay-on-mat* and *'soon'*

Go-to-mat is a more difficult cue for our dogs, as it puts together two behaviours, each of which must be trained separately and then combined.

It is best to start with the last behaviour – the training jargon for this is *back-chaining* (see Section 9.5). The *go-to-mat* cue is taught by starting with our dog being on their mat (*stay-on-mat*), which we facilitate with a chew. The calm behaviour is rewarded with long-lasting chews (such as pigs' ears, lamb's year or kangaroo tails depending on the size of our dog). To teach *stay-on-mat*, we ask our dog to go to their mat and release (meaning allowing them to go off the mat by saying *ok*) after maybe 20-30 seconds. The hand signal is the open-faced palm, as described in Section 9.7.4 for the *stay*. We then gradually extend the time we ask them to stay on their mat. I aim for about 30 minutes maximum.

When our dog loves being on their mat, we start sending them to the mat (*go-to-mat*) by pointing to the mat while we stand just beside it.

We start by showing them the chew, pointing to the mat (same hand), and when they move onto the mat, we *mark* and *reinforce* and give them the chew. Therefore, the signal is pointing to the mat, and once established we add a verbal 'go-to-mat'. We then also add a release cue which can be *ok*, meaning they can get off the mat. We then gradually increase the distance between us and the mat, sending them there from several metres away, then across the room, etc., each time making sure to *mark* and *reinforce*, then release. Very quickly we can send our dog from further and further away to their mat. Once this is reliably on cue (with a success rate of about 80%), we can start introducing distractions, including the doorbell and visitors or during dinner time, always making sure we *mark* and *reinforce* the correct response.

> **Training tip** I use different mats: one which I can take with me (e.g. to the coffee shop) and one that is their bed(s) at home. My aim is that my dogs can rest calmly on their mat at the coffee shop and go to their mats (bed) from anywhere in the house.

Wouldn't it be nice if our dog went to their bed calmly chewing their favourite treat when visitors arrive? This works best if the visitors help by giving them treats when they are on their mat, as our dog both gets a treat and gets to *say hello* to our visitor. If we want to be fancy, we can even transfer the cue from our verbal *go-to-mat* cue to the doorbell. How impressive would that be? To do this, ring the doorbell, immediately followed by the verbal cue *go-to-mat*. *Mark*, *reinforce* and repeat. Once the doorbell becomes the cue, we then can omit our verbal cue. *Go-to-mat* is a great behaviour to manage our teenage dogs who really want to jump on visitors coming to the house. If *go-to-mat* is too difficult a *sit-stay* on their mat or near the door can work as well.

In real life If our dog barks when the doorbell rings, we can get our visitors to call before they come to the house so we can get our treats ready and be prepared for training. Be careful, though: some dogs will catch on to this and they then think that when the phone rings it means someone is coming (and will stand by the door barking). To avoid this, I recommend texting instead. Sometimes they are just too smart for us humans!

The *soon* cue indicates to our dog that the *go-to-mat* will only be short, until we have finished what we are doing. Therefore, *soon* is best introduced once our dog understands the *go-to-mat* and *stay-on-mat* cues and will remain on their mat for at least a few minutes. As with all new cues, we give the new cue first. It looks like this: we say *soon* (new cue) followed by *go-to-mat* (old cue), then we *mark* and *reinforce* and release. With repetitions *soon* will become the cue to go to the mat, relax shortly and wait until we are ready to attend to their needs. We keep the same signal (pointing to the mat) but add *soon* as a verbal cue to distinguish between the two.

Soon is a concept and once dogs understand it, they can generalise to other situations such as the coffee shop or in the car. For example, *soon* can let our dog know on long road trips that we hear them whining to be able to wee and we will pull over as soon as we can. An important factor is that we must be true to our word and give them attention after they have patiently waited. I only use *soon* for a few minutes, or maybe a maximum of ten minutes once trained. If we do not do this, our dog will be left feeling like we do not consider their requests valid, which reduces their trust and they will not learn what *soon* means because we change the goal posts on them.

9.8.2 Crate training

Crate training is an extension of *go-to-mat* training. It follows the same steps but, in the end, we add closing and eventually locking the crate. These steps must be done very gradually so as not to scare or force our dog into an uncomfortable or aversive situation. We start by putting a mat into the crate and asking our dog to go into the crate, with the same visual cue (pointing to the crate with the mat in it). Initially, we might have to lure them into the crate with a chew. In the beginning we just ask them to go in, eat a chew and they can leave at their leisure. Once we feel that they are happy in the crate, we will ask for a short *sit-stay* or *lie-down-stay* facilitated by a chew. After they have finished the chew, we can release them from the crate with *ok* (like how we release them from the mat). We then gradually extend the length of the *sit-stay* or *lie-down-stay* to about 30 minutes.

Once they are ok being in the crate for that amount of time, we start closing the door by about five centimetres but release after maybe five minutes. If they are ok, we can close the door another five centimetres and repeat the procedure, until the door is closed but NOT locked. This means they can push it open when they don't feel comfortable anymore. We then gradually extend the time again with a closed (but not locked) door to whatever time we need them to be in their crate. If all goes well, we then lock the door for a short period of time. If they can do 30 minutes without the crate being locked, we might go back to five minutes and then start building it up again.

Crate training is useful in several situations. For example, it helps if our dogs have to be hospitalised, temporarily boarded in a kennel or travel by air or car or in the case of an evacuation because of a natural disaster (their safe place travels with them). If they are ok and feel safe in a confined crate then it is less stressful when they must stay in (hospital) kennel cages, on holidays or when travelling. Crates can also be a safe place away from enthusiastic children, other pets and people who might take away a toy or chew. Crates are also useful when staying with friends or family, as it gives our dog something comforting and familiar to hang out in when in a strange environment.

Some dog like sleeping in crates during the night, and that can work well. However, we should aim for an open door. This means our dog chooses to sleep in the crate but can leave it they want. Most dogs love to sleep in a confined space (or 'den') when it is cold but want to really stretch out and maybe sleep on a cool floor in summer; it's all about choice (see Section 3.2.4).

A word of warning: some dogs do not take to crate training and it will take a lot of patience and repetitions to get them used to being in a locked crate content, happy and stress free. Keep a close eye on indicators of stress and displacement behaviours (see Section 3.2.3). With work, though, we can convince them that their crate is a desirable place to go when they want to destress, have alone time or enjoy a good chew.

Humans in some countries use crates extensively and, I think, too much. Sweden prohibits crates and they are not very common in Europe. Crates should not be babysitters. Dogs should not be locked into a crate while we are at work all day. I recommend a maximum of two hours in a crate during the day and even less time for puppies. Our aim should be that our dog has free range of the house or yard when home alone. The crate should never be used as punishment or time-out, as that will destroy the comforting and positive associations of their safe space.

 In real life I do crate train most of my puppies, but only overnight. Crate training helps with house-training. Puppies do not soil their beds and they will whine if they need to go to the toilet. This helps to prevent accidents in the house. It means they need to be near where we sleep, so we can hear them and take them out, even in the middle of the night, if necessary. Once they are house-trained, they have free range of the house and sleep where they want to sleep – on their bed, our bed, the couch or the floor.

9.8.3 Teaching the leash

Imagine two different species: one four-legged, close to the ground and one two-legged, standing tall. One sniffs, scratches and wees as they catch up on olfactory neighbourhood gossip and one watches out for traffic, neighbours and kids on skateboards while thinking about what they have to do when they get home again. They are trying to walk down the street at the same pace on a leash. Frankly, neither the dogs nor the humans can manage this without a lot of practice.

Before we start to train leash-walking, we will need a few things: a flat collar, a front-clip harness, treats, patience and a bit of spare time. We will start with teaching the *heel* position first, as our dog will not yet understand the concept of a loose leash. It does not matter which side our dog walks on. Traditionally, dogs are walked on the left as a relic from military training: when holding a gun in their right hand, military personnel needed the dog on their left. I would recommend teaching both sides, although we should start with the one we feel more comfortable with, as the dogs don't really care (in the following example we'll have our dog on our left side, which is convenient for right-handed people).

To get going:

- We put the leash in our right hand. Our dog is on our left side, and the leash connects to them with slack in front of us. We have a handful of treats in our left hand.

- We get our dog's attention by saying their name and showing them the treat, then take the first step, luring them into the correct position (head near our knee). If we have a little dog this is a bit tedious as we are bending over but hang in there as we will get rid of the lure very quickly. As soon as the dog is in the correct position, we *mark* and *reinforce* with the treat. We are making the position near our knee a high-reward zone. We use a lot of lure and treats in the beginning so we can change to a cue very quickly and don't have to keep bending over.

- We repeat and gradually increase the number of steps we are taking, reinforcing after two steps, three steps, seven, ten, etc. If our dog pulls, we stop, ask them to *heel* in the correct position, do a few steps and reinforce. The abstract visual cue is our hand on our hip, which develops from the hand with the lure in front of the dog's muzzle to guide them into the correct position. Once our dog walks in the *heel* position, we add the verbal cue *heel*.

- We do short sessions on our walks, the other part of the walk we let them sniff and explore and be their doggie selves. It helps if we change the set up during our walk to communicate what we are expecting. For example, when they can wander at their own pace, they walk on the harness and when we practice *heel*, they walk on the collar. We can also do short sessions without a lead in the backyard, in the house or in a fenced area.

Similar to this last point, once we start teaching *heel*, we cannot change the goal posts on our dog. This means if we do not have the time or patience to train on a particular day but still need to walk our dog, we need to change something in the setup that clarifies that this is not training time; otherwise we are confusing them. As mentioned, I recommend using a flat collar for *heel* but a front-clip harness if not training and willing to accept a bit of pulling or lagging.

When our dog is reliably in the *heel* position, we can start to move on to loose-leash walking. For this I use the cue *let's-go*. We gradually start relaxing our expectations and let our dog walk a bit ahead or behind as long as there is no tension on the leash. If our dog pulls, we stop, ask them to return to the *heel* position, and *mark* and *reinforce* after a couple of steps in the right position. We then say *let's-go* and keep walking on a loose leash but do not insist on the *heel* position.

Indi doing very well at loose leash walking, next to his human and with no tension on the leash. Picture Grazia Pecoraro.

The most common problems that I have come across are:

- The reinforcement rate is too low. In the beginning we have to reinforce every step. Heeling is boring and difficult for both species to begin with!

- We lure for too long and our dog only does it when they see the treat. We need to phase out lures as soon as possible and change to a cue and a reinforcer.

- The criterion is relaxed too early. Our dog has to understand the heel position as a highly-reinforced zone before they can achieve loose-leash walking.

- We walk straight, boring, predictable paths. If we walk a straight line our dog is very likely to surge ahead because they want to go places, especially teenage dogs. If we are walking curves and figure-eight our path is less predictable and there is less reason to surge ahead.

- The session is too long. We need to keep it short and sweet – don't do training during an entire walk. I recommend starting with one- to two-minute sessions and then gradually training longer; don't do more than five minutes of training at a time.

- We may accidentally end up reinforcing a yo-yo-like action. For example, if our dog pulls and we ask them to *heel* and then reinforce their return, we reward the whole sequence (or behaviour chain; see Sections 8.1.3). Our dog learns to pull—*heel*—pull—*heel*, because we are reinforcing the return to *heel* rather than the correct position. We need to get our dog to walk at least one step in the correct position before we reinforce.

- Walking on a tight leash. If we hold the leash taut, our dog thinks that is what we want. We need a loose leash in order to demonstrate that that is the goal.

Training tip I do not recommend extendable leashes; they are dangerous for both the dog and the humans, they get tangled, cut fingers (and other body parts), and the dog never knows when they reach the end. They also make leashes permanently taut, which means our dog cannot learn the meaning of loose-leash walking. I recommend using a leash that is about 1.2 meters long and double-ended (meaning it has a buckle at either end and can be made shorter or longer, depending on where we walk). I give more range in a quiet neighbourhood and make it shorter in busy areas. I also prefer soft fabric (for comfort) and leashes that are not too heavy (depending on the size of the dog).

Tools such as head halters, check chains or front-clip harnesses are often relied on; I only recommend front-clip harnesses that do not restrict shoulder movement. Check chains and head halters are highly aversive and should not be used at all. They can also cause reactivity or aggression by creating negative associations with other dogs and people. For example, when the dog sees a person or a dog and they start pulling, the check chain will restrict air flow and the head halter will put pressure on the neck and prevent them from looking at the person or dog. Imagine if we were not allowed to look at something we thought was a potential threat or we found unsettling! This will create a negative association which can lead to a host of problems later: barking or lunging or getting scared of other dogs or people when on the leash. This is the last thing we want with a teenage dog! This skill takes a bit of time and patience to train but the result is a dog who walks happily on a collar or back-clip harness.

9.8.4 Meet-and-greet: *Say-hello*

I do not recommend extended greetings between leashed dogs (see Section 6.4.1). It often leads to an altercation because the dogs cannot display appropriate body language and cannot move away. If we do want our dog to meet another dog on-leash, I recommend asking the other human first if their dog is ok to meet (remember: there are plenty of reasons someone may prefer not to let their dog meet others, so we must respect their decision). If we get the go-ahead, we then ask our dog for a *watch-me*, which helps to keep them calm and not rush into the other dog's face. Once they do that, we give them permission to meet the other dog by calmly saying *say-hello*. As our teenage dog is keen to meet anyway, they probably will not need much encouragement or a hand signal to approach. It is best for us humans to stand back and keep the leash loose but short enough to intervene if necessary. I do not recommend patting the other dog but it is fine to have a few polite words with other human while keeping a close eye on the dogs to get ready if things get tense. If they get tense, call them away with a happy voice and increase distance. Pulling them away should be a last resort.

In time, *say-hello* will become the cue for a short meet-and-greet. Follow the three second rule: when they meet, we count to three and move on. We should move on earlier if we can tell they are getting tense. We only allow for three seconds because of the restriction of the leash and limited options to display appropriate body language which might lead to miscommunication. On-leash greetings can become tense quickly and turn into aggression within a split second, so we need to be sure to read our dog's body language.

9.8.5 Tricks

Every dog should learn a few tricks: it is fun, improves our relationship with them and is a great way to keep our teenage dog's brain busy. Another main reason for trick-training is that it improves our training technique. We are often tense when we try to teach our dogs basic things like *sit* or *lie-down*. But, as soon as we teach tricks – for example *shake-paw, spin, weave-through-my-legs* or *sit-pretty* – we all lighten up, have fun and engage on a different level with our dogs. Because us humans have changed our mind set – we are more engaging and start to have fun – the dogs pick up on this and become more engaged and are keener to work and play with their humans. It also seems that when we realise that our own attitude and behaviour influences our dogs, we are more likely to have a positive attitude with the 'boring' but necessary obedience behaviours. Like in any other relationship, as soon as we relax and have fun, everything works better.

Most tricks – like *spin, sit-pretty, take-a-bow,* and *weave-through-my-legs* – should be taught with a lure. This means we put the food in front of the dog's face and guide them into the correct position. As soon as they are in the position, we add the verbal cue and *mark* and *reinforce*. We lure a few times and then we pretend to have the food in the hand but reinforce from the other hand. After a few more repetitions they do what we want with just a hand signal.

Spin

We lure our dog to stand in front of us, facing to the right, then lure them to move in a counter-clockwise circle away from us. The key is to start very close in front of our feet and lure them away from us without having to bend over too much. Our hand should almost be touching their nose, and we use our lure to draw a circular line for them to follow. Lots of dogs find it scary when we bend over them too much but if we keep it positive, they will get used to it very quickly. The hand signal is a spin motion with our hand. Teach both sides and we can call one *spin* and the other *twirl* or similar.

Sit-pretty

We ask our dog to *sit* facing us. We bring a lure very close over their head and move it backwards behind them so they lift their front feet off the ground but their rear end stays on the floor. It is like *sit* but the front legs are off the ground. They look like big meerkats when doing that, and it always makes people smile. The hand signal is a flat hand (as with *sit*) going past their head.

Take-a-bow

Our dog stands facing us. We bring a treat between their front legs, close to the floor and towards their chest. To get the treat they will need to bend their front legs, hopefully while hind legs stay up. Some dogs will go into a *lie-down*. To avoid this, try to *mark* when their rear end is still in the air and move the lure hand with away very quickly. The hand signal is a bow motion towards our dog and our hand pointing between their legs.

Weave(-through-my-legs)

Our dog stands facing us. We reach through our legs and lure them between and around our left leg and then the right leg in a figure-eight. Some dogs might find this a bit a scary and it helps if we teach them to go through our legs first by throwing a treat through our legs, behind us. The only thing they need to do in the beginning is to run through our legs to get the treat. Most dogs will feel comfortable with this quickly. Having a treat in each hand will help with the flow and our co-ordination. Once they have learnt the trick, it is often enough for us to stand with our legs apart and give the verbal cue *weave;* no hand signal is required.

Shake-paw

Teaching to *shake-paw* we use a different approach than luring. We hold the treat in our closed fist in front of our dog, at about the level of their chest. Most dogs will try to get to the treat and will start pawing our hand. As soon as their paw moves towards our fist, we open our hand and they get the treat. Once they lift the paw reliably and touch our closed fist, we switch to pretending that the food is still in that hand and as soon as their paw touches our fist, we open that hand and give them the treat from our other hand. The hand cue is the outstretched flat palm facing up, we can then add the verbal cue *shake-paw.* Most dogs will not confuse the *sit* cue with the *hand-touch* or *shake-paw* cue because the context is different. When we ask for a *shake-paw* we are lower (more on their level, so we are able to shake 'paws' with them) which indicates to them that this is different to the *sit* cue where we normally stand straight up or the *hand-touch* where we mostly stand next to them or in front of them.

9.8.6 Husbandry behaviours

These are behaviours we teach our dogs to take the stress out of vet visits and their regular upkeep. This includes social vet visits, stepping onto a scale, head rest, nail trimming, ear and eye drops, taking pills and muzzle training. Brushing and grooming fall into this category, too. With all these behaviours we will break them down into small achievable steps and gradually teach our dogs to accept them and, hopefully, participate willingly.

We should check our dogs daily for ticks (if we are in a tick area) and at least every few days for other injuries, bumps and lumps to make sure they are ok and are not in pain or discomfort. Make sure to check between their toes, in their ears, their gums and teeth to ensure they are not inflamed or irritated. This can be part of a relaxing massage and grooming session.

Cleaning teeth

I really have not seen any of my clients be successful with brushing their dog's teeth. It just seems a difficult thing to teach and too tedious for most of us, especially given there are easy options out there (even if we don't want to feed them bones). There are dental sticks or other chews such as kangaroo jerky or tails, pigs' ears or lamb ears that help with keeping their teeth clean. You can also buy special dental pet food, and/or have their teeth professionally cleaned by the vet.

In real life While I do not generally give advice on nutrition, I think bones go a long way to keep teeth clean. I will admit that I do not brush my dogs' teeth. Because they are on a raw food diet with a lot of bones, I have never had to. None of my dogs every needed dental work even at 14 years of age. But every dog is different, so make sure and do your own research on this!

Veterinary hospitals and practices

A difficult part of life for most dogs is the vet visit. All dogs need to go to the vet when they are sick or injured and when they need their annual check-up or vaccination. It is extremely stressful for our dog (and us) if our dog is overly scared and becomes a shivering mess at the vet. It is normal for dogs to be a little stressed or apprehensive at the vet given the strange sights, smells and sounds – but if they are petrified on arrival it is heartbreaking to watch and it can be difficult for the vet to diagnose or provide treatment.

Luckily, we can do something about this with a lot of social visits when our dogs are puppies and teenagers. We need to take our young dogs to the vet regularly and start social vet visits early to prevent them from becoming fearful in this environment. I recommend social vet visits on a weekly basis for puppies and teenage dogs.

We start with just walking into the clinic, giving our dog a few treats and leaving again. We repeat this a few times until they appear to be enjoying going in. We then ask the nurses or receptionist to give them treats. If our dog has experience with getting on objects, we can ask them to get on the scale and give them a treat for doing so. Once they are relaxed, we can start going into the treatment rooms and meet the vet.

We need to make the vet visit as pleasant as possible by being generous with our treats and choosing procedures that are less invasive. There are more-and-more vets who offer a version of 'fear free pets' vet visits (check for these vets in your area)[90]. Additionally, a well-run puppy class at the vet of your choice can help to create a positive association, too.

 In real life My otherwise outgoing, confident and happy dog Shellbe – an eight-year old German shorthaired pointer – was one of those dogs who arrived at the vet in a state of panic. Despite doing a lot of social vet visits at an early age, it only took one bad experience to spoil it for her. At eight months of age she received a very stinging and painful injection for diarrhoea. At this stage I did not know that it was painful and the vet did not bother mentioning it. In addition, Shellbe was probably in a secondary fear phase. I have done uncountable social visits and a lot of counter-conditioning since and we are now using less invasive procedures and less restraint. She still does not like it, but she now can at least keep it together. I have taught her to use a headrest on my shoulder when she gets stressed and we are at a stage where she will put her head on my shoulder, stand still and can have a vaccination or a blood test done without a panic attack. In hindsight we should have tried a different, less-invasive treatment for the diarrhoea first. The nasal spray for kennel cough is similarly unpleasant. A few years ago, I insisted that the vet source a vaccine that could be administered in another way, preferably oral. After a bit of discussion, they investigated and found an oral vaccine. When I later asked for this to be used with my other dog, they told me that it now had become standard at their clinic and that they did not use the nasal spray anymore because it is too scary and unpleasant for most dogs.

Step-on

Teaching our dogs to step onto the scales at the vet starts with a plank at home. This is the first step towards teaching them to step onto unusual things. We can use luring for this: hold a treat in front of their face and guide them onto the plank. If they are not comfortable with this, we might only ask for the front feet to begin with and then gradually ask them to put their hind feet on. The hand signal is pointing to the plank/scales, similar to *go-to-mat*. If they have a *go-to-mat* cue, putting a mat on the plank/scales to start with can help. Once they are comfortable stepping onto things, we can add a verbal cue with it, like *step-on*. We can also practice this on our walks by asking our dogs to *step-on* to different surfaces and *mark* and *reinforce* when they do. Once our dog understands the *step-on* cue at home and is comfortable at the vet, we can ask them to *step-on* to the vet scale. Keep it short in the beginning: we should lure them into stepping onto it, then allow them to step off. Then we can ask for them to *stay* there for a few seconds and gradually we can ask them to spend more time on the scale.

 In real life One dog I know of is so well-trained at getting on the scale that he just hangs out on it when his humans are in the vet waiting room. It is confusing to him, when other dogs try and get on it and he will have to be asked to get off, because he knows he's supposed to go stand on it.

Head-rest

We teach our dog to rest their head in our hand or on a chair as a way to teach accepting touch from the vet or other health professional; it is their way of expressing consent. Throughout teaching *head-rest*, we must always be vigilant of our dog's comfort, and respect that they can say 'no' and withdraw consent to be touched (*head-rest* is linked to start-button behaviours and choice; see Section 3.2.4). This means they have more control over what happens to them. If they leave their head in our hand or on the chair, they are saying it is *ok* for the vet to proceed. If they take their head away, it means *no* and the vet needs to stop what they are doing. Using a chair or the hand is a personal preference, as both work the same. If using a chair, I recommend putting a towel on the chair so we can take the towel to the vet and they still understand the behaviour in a different context.

Unfortunately, sometimes there is an emergency and things need to be done before we can obtain our dog's consent and condition the vet to be a non-scary place. There are different ways of dealing with this. If we are doing routine things like injections that are not very time-sensitive, I would stick to the training plan and just defer for a few days or a week and do a lot more training to get them ready. In an emergency situation there are medications that can help or sedation. Talk to your vet about what is appropriate to prevent a negative association between them and your dog.

There is also a 'phenomenon' that works in our favour, called *latent inhibition*. This means if our dog has had a lot of good experiences at the vet, one bad experience will not completely ruin it. They most likely will maintain a positive attitude despite the aversive procedure. But, we also need to be aware that there is 'one event learning' or 'flashbulb memories' (see Section 4.5) and that despite all our best efforts one negative experience can ruin all of our hard work in creating positive associations. These 'one event learning' events are extremely difficult to overcome.

To teach *head-rest* we use shaping, by breaking the behaviour down into small steps. The first step is *look-at-hand/chair*, which we *mark* and *reinforce*. Then we move on to *approach-hand/chair* (*mark* and *reinforce*), *touch-hand/chair* (*mark* and *reinforce*) and finally *leave-chin-in-hand/ chair* (*mark* and *reinforce*). Once they understand that we want their head to rest in our hand or on the chair we add the verbal cue *head-rest*. Check Youtube for a step-by-step video on teaching *head-rest*[91].

 In real life Chillax needed to go to the emergency vet because he was vomiting, very lethargic and had pale gums. I was very worried and rushed him there. By the time we got there he had perked up and looked kind of ok, but I still wanted him checked out. This was not our normal vet and Chillax was a bit skittish to start with. The vet was rather impatient and said 'If he will not stand still, I will get a nurse to restrain him.' I replied 'No way!' That slowed things down (remember, you are your dog's advocate!). Instead of a *head-rest* I asked Chillax for an obedience *stand-stay*, restraining him slightly with his harness. He could do it and let the vet take his temperature, use the stethoscope, feel his abdomen and give him an antihistamine injection. There was treats galore for this performance. I did not ask for the *head-rest* because he was too stressed, he would not have given consent and I did not want to jeopardise the trust. If it had still been an emergency, I would probably have asked them to sedate Chillax to prevent him having to be poked and prodded while restrained. But these decisions need to be made in discussion with our treating vet. A fear-free vet is better equipped to help with these decisions.

Nail trimming

There are two ways to go about trimming our dog's nails, which should be done on a regular basis. We can use a desensitising counter-conditioning process or teach them to do their own nails on a scratch board.

If we use the first approach, we start by showing them the nail clipper (*mark* and *reinforce* to create a positive association). If they approach the clipper, we *mark* and *reinforce*; if they sniff the clipper, we *mark* and *reinforce*. We do these 'baby steps' until they associate the nail clipper

with treats. At the same time, we teach them to p
hand (*mark* and *reinforce*), just like we taught the
then hold the paw a bit longer (*mark* and *reinforce*),
nail (*mark* and *reinforce*), and then touch their nai
reinforce). Once our dog voluntarily offers their paw
then introduce the idea of the nail clipper being near their paw. We
take the clipper close to their nail (*mark* and *reinforce*), we touch the
nail with the clipper (*mark* and *reinforce*), we pretend to clip (*mark*
and *reinforce*). We repeat this until we can clip the nail without them
pulling away.

Personally, I prefer to teach my dogs to do their nails themselves by
teaching them to use a scratch board. This makes the process less
stressful and gives them more autonomy to participate. It is possible to
teach the use of scratch board quite quickly, as can be seen in an online
video[92]. We start by using the *shake-paw* cue (flat hand palm facing up)
to get them to put their paw into our hand. Once they put their paw
up reliably, we ask for *shake-paw* but instead of holding the hand still,
we lower our hand to an almost vertical position. We then put a postie
note on our hand, so they now touch the postie note when we ask for
shake-paw. Then we use a sandpaper instead of the postie note. Once
they are comfortable touching the vertical sandpaper and scratch their
nails, we glue the sandpaper to a chopping board (or similar) and hold
the board in front of them. They are now scratching and trimming their
nails on the board. While this might sound tedious, if you watch the
video it become clear and it is not difficult.

Ear/eye drops

Ear/eye-drop administration requires desensitising our dog to the experience. Giving medication via drops can be hard if our dogs do not co-op-
erate and have to be restrained/forced to get it done. To teach our dogs
to accept ear drops, we start with getting them used to our touch and
our manipulation of their ears. We ask our dog to *sit* and then we place

and near their ear (*mark* and *reinforce*); we then touch their ear (*mark* and *reinforce*). We keep increasing the length of time and ways that we touch their ears until they are comfortable with it (which we can assess by reading their behaviour). We then show them the medicine bottle for them to look at (*mark* and *reinforce*) and sniff (*mark* and *reinforce*). We hold the bottle closer to their face (*mark* and *reinforce*), hold it to their ear (*mark* and *reinforce*), touch the outside of their ear (*mark* and *reinforce*), etc. We do a few repetitions at each step and only move on if they are comfortable and relaxed. If at any point they are reluctant, we need to go back one step and make it easier.

We do the same with their eyes. This is a bit more difficult as the eyes do not lend themselves for easy patting as the ears do. But, most dogs like a bit of an eye rub with our flat hands. We then very gently start touching the area around their eyes (*mark* and *reinforce*), then the eyelid (*mark* and *reinforce*), then we start lifting the eyelid (*mark* and *reinforce*), holding it slightly longer and longer (*mark* and *reinforce*). Then we introduce the medicine bottle, bringing it gradually closer until we can apply the medicine. We go very slowly and *mark* and *reinforce* every step. We need to practice this not only when we need to give ear/eye drops but also on an ongoing basis so our dogs participate willingly.

Taking pills

There are at least two ways to go about giving our dogs their medication. It often works if we have the pills hidden in treats and randomly use them in a training session. We just hide the pill in one of the treats we use in training. Note that soft treats are best for this (cheese, banana or whatever else we can sink a pill into). We ask for a behaviour they know well like *sit* or a trick (*mark* and *reinforce*), starting with a few plain treats and then the one with the pill, followed immediately with another one without a pill. This works most of the time! Another option is to teach our dogs to catch treats when we throw them, since they do not have much time to process or chew. This is the same procedure: let them catch a few without pills, then one with a pill, immediately throwing the next one. Often, they don't even realise that they took the pill.

Muzzle training

Dogs, contrary to humans, do not have a negative preconception with the muzzle (although they can develop one with negative experiences). For them it is just another piece of equipment if introduced carefully. It is well worth training our dog on a muzzle because, in the case of an injury, it will make a vet visit much less stressful. If our dog is injured and in pain, even the most placid dog might bite and make treatment difficult or impossible. In these cases, the vet will use a muzzle to protect themselves. If our dog is used to the muzzle then we have one less stressor. If they are not, then the muzzle will make an already-stressful situation worse.

Muzzle training requires desensitising and counter-conditioning. It works similar to eye and ear drops, but it is easier. We start by showing them the muzzle (*mark* and *reinforce*). We bring the muzzle a bit closer, they might look at it (*mark* and *reinforce*) or sniff it (*mark* and *reinforce*). Then we put a few treats in the muzzle and let them eat the treats. Eventually they will put their nose in it (*mark* and *reinforce*) and keep it there for longer (*mark* and *reinforce*). We then bring the strap behind their head (*mark* and *reinforce*), close the strap (*mark* and *reinforce*), and gradually build up the duration of it staying on. Every step is repeated and reinforced as many times as necessary so they don't get stressed and it is a positive experience. For more information on muzzle training check out the Muzzle Up Project[93].

Brushing

Some dogs need to be brushed, especially if long-haired or during shedding seasons. Some dogs like this, while others will run away from the sight of the brush. To teach our dogs to enjoy brushing we can do the following steps: show them the brush (*mark* and *reinforce*), let them approach the brush (*mark* and *reinforce*), let them sniff the brush (*mark* and *reinforce*), bring the brush closer to their body (*mark* and *reinforce*), touch their neck with the brush (*mark* and *reinforce*), touch other body parts with the brush (*mark* and *reinforce*), brush gently for one second (*mark* and *reinforce*), two seconds (*mark* and *reinforce*), etc.

Part of this aversion to brushing is due to our own behaviours. We often don't brush our dogs in an enjoyable way; slamming the brush down on their head and then dragging it along their spin is unpleasant or painful. Using soft brushes, avoid tugging their hair and being aware of body parts they don't like being brushed is important. We need to change how we think about this. Instead of wrestling our dogs to remove hair we should see it as a chance to give them a massage and gently untangle their hair. We should go slow and considerate. If done properly brushing can be a pleasant bonding time for humans and dogs. I know some people who love brushing dogs and some who don't. If you don't like it, I recommend a short-coated dog who doesn't need brushing.

9.9 Summary

We use operant conditioning to teach new behaviours and respondent conditioning (including counterconditioning and desensitising) to create more positive associations between stimuli and responses. In order to successfully train, we should start with easy behaviours and then gradually add in distance, duration and distractions. If things go wrong, we interrupt, redirect, and reinforce alternative behaviours. It will help if we manage the environment appropriately, partly so we can be careful about creating undesirable behaviour chains. Using life rewards that are contingent on an intimate knowledge of our dog's preferences will enhance our training beyond just providing treats or toys. Learning the basics and more advanced behaviours will help us and our dogs navigate daily life. It will also help our dogs to go places with us, join our favourite activities and enjoy more freedom. Some of the more advanced concepts will reduce stress during vet visits and help with caring for our dogs in a co-operative and positive way.

Chapter 10
Conclusion – Where to go from here?

Yes, teenage dogs can be difficult and can make us want to tear our hair out. But they are also fun, exciting, loving and they really try their very best! We humans need to try our best, too, and take these challenging months for what they are: a phase everyone has to go through. It is well worth it when the result is a confident, calm and well-behaved friend. The main point we need to remind ourselves of is that our teenage dogs are not being difficult on purpose. Their brain is under construction and they have a hard time processing information accurately and making good decisions, given the lack of impulse control and emotional reactivity. We need to help them make these good decisions!

Considering our dogs as our friends or family – and treating them with respect and compassion – should be our aim. We need to recognise that they have their own goals and preferences. This will take time, patience, realistic expectations, clear communication, trust and options for choice. While we do not know exactly what our teenage dogs feel, we can be certain that they have feelings, and many of these would be similar to our own. These feelings need to be taken into consideration – e.g. rather than yelling at our dog for excessive barking, we should consider what emotion they are feeling that is leading to that behaviour. Critical anthropomorphism is not a 'sin' anymore but is, in fact, an appropriate way to understand our teenage dogs (and all animals).

We need to approach the teenage life stage similar to how we approach puppyhood: with accurate information, professional guidance and best practice teaching methods. This will not only help our teenage dog but make it easier for us humans as well. Teaching our dog using positive reinforcement (instead of 'dominating' them) and giving them some choice over the outcome of their actions will make for a much better relationship and much better results in the long run, especially since we are treating the cause (rather than the symptoms) of their discomfort/misbehaviour. Positive reinforcement methods are best practice and the science has been settled: positive methods work better and with less side effects. Don't be tempted by the promise of a 'quick fix'; there is no such thing!

Living with our dogs is a huge commitment which includes a lifetime of socialisation so they can live successfully in our modern human world. Teaching our dogs how to behave in a world that is not made for them is not optional, but, rather our obligation and responsibility as humans. Part of this obligation is that we need to keep our teenage dog's brain and body fit and engaged, especially if they are left home alone regularly. There are challenges with providing them with appropriate mental and physical stimulation, but daily training and social outings will make all the difference. Additionally, teaching our dog (and ourselves) to recognise and value being calm will help; 'down time' is important and we can and should promote calmness. We can overcome the daily challenges with enrichment and responding appropriately to both 'bad' and 'good' behaviour.

Using operant and respondent conditioning we teach our dog what the appropriate and desirable behaviours are. When all goes wrong, we can calmly redirect to something more appropriate and take the opportunity to ensure we are being clear about what behaviour we would prefer.

If you find yourself despairing, get professional help. Teenage dog training classes are becoming more common and are a great way to get information and meet other humans in the same situation. But, make sure you are engaging a qualified and accredited trainer. As mentioned, the dog training industry is still unregulated and too many so-called 'dog trainers' have no qualification to their name and are not a member of a reputable association with a code of ethics. You need to check their qualification first! A Certificate IV in Companion Animal Services (or equivalent) should be the minimum standard. An accreditation and membership with a reputable association is another must. There are three organisations in Australia that have trainers' directory with qualified and accredited trainers: The Pet Professional Guild Australia[94], the Delta Institute[95] and The Association of Pet Dog Trainers (APDT) Australia[96]. If you are in the USA, the article *How To Choose a Dog Trainer* by Todd is a great starting point[97].

Remember: once our dog has reached social maturity, we tend to forget these difficult months and hopefully we will spend the next ten years or more enjoying each other's company! In the meantime, I recommend a healthy dose of patience, humour and willingness to meet your friend halfway.

About Barbara Hodel

Over the last 13 years, I have professionally helped thousands of humans and their teenage dogs to get through that challenging teenage phase. I wrote this book because I want to share the lessons I have learnt – and the knowledge I have gained – with a wider audience so you and your dog can develop a lasting bond and live together harmoniously!

Dogs I have learnt from

I have a long, personal history training my own dogs. I had a Dalmatian as I child, but my passion for dogs started when I met my husband in 1993, who had just adopted Ajtano. Ajtano was an older large, mixed-breed dog with an interesting history. As with my husband, it was love at first sight, and we developed a deep bond. He came to Switzerland as a puppy with a well-meaning person who had found him wandering the streets in Spain. She could not keep him and he moved from home to home until my husband adopted him when he was about ten years old. Perhaps because of this, he remained an independent dog who loved his humans but never forgot his early history of fending from himself. He once got lost on the other side of the city wandering off a building site where he had been with my husband. He found his way home, which required crossing the entire city – including busy four-lane roads, dodging buses, trams and pedestrians. I am sure he took the tram for the last part of his journey (I often took him into the city centre by tram for outings and shopping, so he knew that part of the way home)! What an amazing thing to do. I also taught this old dog new tricks, as my first foray into dog training, and he lived a happy life to over 14 years.

About Barbara

When we moved to Australia, we soon adopted a German Shepherd-cross, Soma. She was only six-months old when we got her, but we were her third home. We got her right when the teenage phase hit and while we had a few challenging months, she grew into a well-adjusted dog and became a much-loved member of our family. She was my first agility dog and we did well, despite both of us being complete beginners in this sport.

Soma got me interested in dog training, but Zorbas was the start of my interest in dog behaviour and the beginning of my passion to help dogs and their humans reach their full potential. Zorbas, a Kelpie-cross I got from a friend in 2004, did not 'perform' in agility how I expected him to. He was not only a challenging dog during his teenage months but he was anxious, too. He did not cope with the competition environment or any high-arousal situations. I had to adjust my expectations, stop competing and help him cope with a world he found trying. Because of him, I started studying dog behaviour which has allowed me to now understand what it means to live with a challenging teenage dog and a dog who finds the world a scary place. With a lot of patience, positive reinforcement training and a relationship based on trust, he lived a happy life (without competitions) to 14.5 years; enjoying outings, training and holidays until the very end.

I am a registered breeder with Dogs NSW and have successfully bred and raised confident and well-adjusted German short-haired pointer puppies. I compete successfully on the highest level in Agility and Rally Obedience with Shellbe (short for 'she'll be right'), my eight-year-old German short-haired pointer. My young dog Chillax, another German short-haired pointer (from Shellbe's last litter), is just starting out but did come 3rd in his very first Rally O trial at 14 months and won his first Rally O trial when he was two years old.

My professional dog skills

In pursuit of helping others to learn how to deal with the teenage dog challenge and maintain a healthy, respectful relationship with their dogs, I quit the corporate world in 2007 and completed a Certificate IV in Companion Animal Services as a Delta-qualified instructor. My dog-training business Goodog Positive Dog Training (www.goodog.com.au), on the Northern Beaches of Sydney, took off quickly and I have never looked back. At Goodog, my small team of highly-qualified and passionate trainers and I provide dog-training classes for puppies, manners classes for rescue and teenage dogs, as well as workshops for typical teenage problems (such as recall and walking on the leash). We also offer fun agility classes and do in-home consultations for problem behaviours and puppy set-ups.

Prior to starting Goodog, I had started instructing in a club environment over 17 years ago but felt that the harsh training methods still used in clubs were not right and something was missing. The dog-training world was still firmly in the hands of law-enforcement officers and army-dog handlers, who use a heavy-handed and dominance-based approach. This means they used commands and if the dog did not comply, they forced them into submission; physical punishment was accepted and just a 'normal' part of training. The well-being of the dogs was secondary to compliance and of no real concern to the trainers. With my background in adult education, it just did not make sense to me to use force and compulsion to teach dogs. There had to be a better way!

The Delta course provided a great starting point for my knowledge of dog-training, but it was not delivering the science on behaviour I felt was needed to change the way we train dogs. I found what I was looking for in my studies for a Diploma in Canine Behaviour Science and Technology at the Companion Animal Sciences Institute in Canada (graduated in 2015). This experience provided me with the theory for my science-based, ethical and humane approach to dog training and behaviour. Science and critical anthropomorphism are the basis of my dog-training advice in my daily work and in this book.

I have taken this theory and applied it through all aspects of my interactions with dogs and their humans. For example, I am now the president of the Pet Professional Guild Australia. The Pet Professional Guild Australia is a not-for-profit membership organisation for people with pets and trainers using force-free methods that advocates a science-based and best-practice approach to training of all species.

I did have a life before dogs and finding my current vocation and passion. I hold a Master's degree in Modern European History and Economics from the University of Bern (Switzerland) and a Master of Business Administration (MBA) from Southern Cross University Lismore (Australia). I have in-depth experience in adult education and training, having taught high-school and university students in Bern, college students in Sydney, as well as middle- and top-management employees of a large public corporation in Switzerland. I also worked in management positions in marketing for Swiss Federal Railways and the Canton of Berne.

My experiences – both personal and professional – have prepared me for teaching dogs and their humans in a positive and science-based way. Teaching students or managers is not different from teaching humans and their dogs. The only difference is that we stopped using force with humans decades ago, which means it has never really made sense to me to use it in dog training – and I never have!

Contact

If you would like to share your thoughts on the book or teenage dogs with me, I can be contacted via the website www.goodog.com.au, Facebook page https://www.facebook.com/goodogpositivedogtraining or e-mail barbara@goodog.com.au.

Acknowledgments

Thanks to Ueli, who has always believed that I can do it! Thanks to Virginia Pennefather for giving me a chance very early in my dog training career and for being the test reader. Thanks to my friends Grazia Pecoraro, Jess Sandstrom and Le Hammer who helped with photos of their teenage dogs. Thanks to Rebecca Hendershott who was much more than an editor and supported me throughout my first book project!

References

American Heritage Dictionary of the English Language 2016 'Operant conditioning' Houghton Mifflin Harcourt Publishing Company (https://www.thefreedictionary.com/operant+conditioning)

Anderson E 2015 'Fallout from the use of aversives' *Eileen and Dogs* blog (https://eileenanddogs.com/fallout-aversives-punishment-negative-reinforcement/)

Anderson E 2019 (21 Oct) 'Why "red zone dogs" need positive reinforcement training' *Eileen and Dogs* blog (https://eileenanddogs.com/blog/2014/09/19/effects-punishment/)

Arnold J 2016 *Love is all you need: The revolutionary bond-based approach to educating your dog* Random House Publishing Group: New York, NY

Association of Pet Dog Trainers Australia Inc. n.d.(a) 'APDT Code of Ethics' *APDT* website (https://www.apdt.com.au/about-us/apdt-code-of-ethics.html)

Association of Pet Dog Trainers Australia Inc. n.d.(b) 'APDT Trainers Directory' *APDT* website (https://www.apdt.com.au/trainers-directory/find-a-trainer.html)

Australian Veterinary Association n.d. 'Reward-based training: A guide for dog trainers' *AVA* website (https://www.ava.com.au/library-resources/other-resources/behaviour-resources-for-veterinarians/)www.deltainstitute.edu.au

Balance Behaviour n.d. 'Biting and chewing' *Balance Behaviour: Dog Fulfilment & Owner Confidence* website (http://www.balancebehaviour.org/detaiul)

Bangasser DA and Shors TJ 2010 'Critical brain circuits at the intersection between stress and learning' *Neuroscience Biobehavioral Reviews* 34(8):1223-1233 (https://doi.org/10.1016/j.neubiorev.2010.02.002)

Bekoff M 2008 *The emotional lives of animals: A leading scientist explores animal joy, sorrow, and empathy – and why they matter* New World Library: Novato, CA

Bekoff M 2019a (29 Jan) 'Science shows positive reward-based dog training is best' *Psychology Today* https://www.psychologytoday.com/us/blog/animal-emotions/201901/science-shows-positive-reward-based-dog-training-is-best)

Bekoff M 2019b (31 Dec) '2020 hindsight demands changes in animal-human interactions' *Psychology Today* (https://www.psychologytoday.com/us/blog/animal-emotions/201912/2020-hindsight-demands-changes-in-animal-human-interactions)

References

Bender A and Strong E 2019 *Canine enrichment for the real world: Making it a part of your dog's daily life* Dogwise Publishing: Wenatchee, WA

Berns GS 2016 (17 April) 'Neurobiology of self-control in dogs' *Psychology Today* (https://www.psychologytoday.com/au/blog/plus2sd/201604/neurobiology-self-control-in-dogs)

Berns GS, Brooks AM, Spivak M 2015 'Scent of the familiar: An fMRI study of canine brain responses to familiar and unfamiliar human and dog odors' *Behavioural Processes* 110:37-46 (https://doi.org/10.1016/j.beproc.2014.02.011)

Berns GS and Cook PF 2016 'Why did the dog walk into the MRI' *Current Directions in Psychological Science* 25(5): 363-369 (https://doi.org/10.1177%2F0963721416665006)

Brucks D, Essler JL, Marshall-Pescini S, Range F 2016 'Inequity aversion negatively affects tolerance and contact-seeking behaviours towards partner and experimenter' *PLOS One* 11(4): e0153799 (https://doi.org/10.1371/journal.pone.0153799)

Burghardt GM 2007 'Critical anthropomorphism, uncritical anthropocentrism, and naïve nominalism' *Comparative Cognition & Behavior Reviews* 2:136-138 (https://doi.org/10.3819/ccbr.2008.20009)

Carlisle-Frank P and Frank JM 2016 'Owners, guardians, and owner-guardians: Differing relationships with pets' *Anthrozoös* 19(3): 225-242 (https://doi.org/10.2752/089279306785415574)

Cattet J 2013 (16 Sept) 'Animal emotions – the driving force behind our dog's behaviors' *Smart Animal Training* blog (http://blog.smartanimaltraining.com/2013/09/16/animal-emotions-the-driving-force-behind-our-dogs-behaviors/)

Cherry K 2019 (14 May) 'Classical vs. operant conditioning: 2 important concepts central to behavioural psychology' *VeryWellMind.com* (https://www.verywellmind.com/classical-vs-operant-conditioning-2794861)

Cook PF 2017 'Studying dog emotion beyond expression and without concern for feeling: Commentary on Kujala on *Canine Emotions*' *Animal Sentience* 14(15) (https://animalstudiesrepository.org/cgi/viewcontent.cgi?article=1282&context=animsent)

Dahl M 2016 (22 April) 'Maybe it's time to take animal feelings seriously' *The Feed* (https://www.sbs.com.au/news/the-feed/maybe-it-s-time-to-take-animal-feelings-seriously?fbclid=IwAR3piSctigsxsPe8VORjfgDlADwIwXgTQUCxz5ZITU-7gAGw7oSx0tTrIXag)

Delta Institute n.d.(a) 'Code of Ethics' found on *Delta Institute* 'About Us' webpage (https://www.deltainstitute.edu.au/about-us)

Delta Institute n.d.(b) 'Find a trainer' *Delta Institute* website https://www.deltainstitute.edu.au/find-a-trainer

De Rosa F 2018 'How to create a sensory garden for your dog' *AustralianDogLover.com* (https://www.australiandoglover.com/2018/12/how-to-create-sensory-garden-for-your.html)

de Waal F 2017 *Are we smart enough to know how smart animals are?* W. W. Norton: London, UK

Dog Knowledge 2018 (27 Nov) 'Dog-Dog play' *Facebook* (https://www.facebook.com/dogknowledge/videos/2088715597859355/)

Edmonds M 2008 (26 Aug) 'Are teenage brains really different from adult brains?' *Howstuffworks.com* (https://science.howstuffworks.com/life/inside-the-mind/human-brain/teenage-brain1.htm)

Farricelli A 2016 (6 Nov) '13 negative effects of aversive dog training methods' *DogDiscoveries.com* (https://dogdiscoveries.com/aversive-dog-training-methods/)

Frederick E 2019 (2 Sept) 'Humans haven't just changed what dogs look like – we've altered the very structure of their brains' *Science* (https://www.sciencemag.org/news/2019/09/humans-haven-t-just-changed-what-dogs-look-we-ve-altered-very-structure-their-brains)

Garrett S n.d. 'Give this easy game a try: ItsYerChoice' *Susan Garrett* website (https://susangarrettdogagility.com/2018/06/why-choice-is-the-critical-key-to-a-great-dog/)

Garvey M, Stella J, Croney C 2016 (March) 'Implementing environmental enrichment for dogs' *Purdue Extension* (https://extension.purdue.edu/extmedia/VA/VA-13-W.pdf)

Ginman L 2013 *The art of introducing dogs: A guide for conducting dog to dog introductions* Balboa Press: Bloomington, IN

Goodog channel 2016a (17 July) 'Close the door!' *Youtube* (https://www.youtube.com/watch?v=wGxFI3PDTNA&list=UUCA8jdrq6Xc779HXJUhtmGw&index=27)

Goodog channel 2016b (18 Oct) 'head rest' *YouTube* (https://www.youtube.com/watch?v=MHF_ku6YOtY)

Goodog channel 2016c (18 Dec) 'Puppy's first day at home' *Youtube* (https://www.youtube.com/watch?v=yDp2sjmQxI0)

Goodog Positive Dog Training 2017 (29 Nov) 'nail filing' *Facebook* (https://www.facebook.com/goodogpositivedogtraining/videos/1676238659063444/)

References

Haraway D 2003 *The companion species manifesto: Dogs, people, and significant otherness* Prickly Paradigm Press: Chicago, IL

Hare B and Tomasello M 2005 'Human-like social skills in dogs?' *TRENDS in Cognitive Sciences* 9(9):439-444 (https://doi.org/10.1016/j.tics.2005.07.003)

Harris CR and Prouvost C 2014 'Jealousy in dogs' *PLOS One* 9(7): e94597 (https://doi.org/10.1371/journal.pone.0094597)

Herron ME, Kirby-Madden TM, Lord LK 2014 'Effects of environmental enrichment on the behaviour of shelter dogs' *Journal of the American Veterinary Medical Association* 244(6):687-692 (https://doi.org/10.2460/javma.244.6.687)

Horowitz A 2009a *Inside of a dog: What dogs see, smell, and know* Scribner: London, UK

Horowitz A 2009b 'Disambiguating the "guilty look": Salient prompts to a familiar dog behaviour' *Behavioural Processes* 81(3):447-452 (https://doi.org/10.1016/j.beproc.2009.03.014)

Hunter M 2016 (6 Jan) 'Training concepts: What is shaping?' *DogTrainingology.com* (https://www.dogtrainingology.com/concepts/shaping-behavior-definition/#Part1)

Joëls M, Pu Z, Wiegert O, Oitz MS, Krugers HJ 2006 'Learning under stress: How does it work?' *Trends in Cognitive Sciences* 10:152-158 (https://doi.org/10.1016/j.tics.2006.02.002)

Kaminski J, Waller BM, Diogo R, Hartstone-Rose A, Burrows AM 2019 'Evolution of facial muscle anatomy in dogs' *PNAS* 116(29):14677-14681 (https://doi.org/10.1073/pnas.1820653116)

Kaulfuß P and Mills DS 2008 'Neophilia in domestic dogs (*Canis familiaris*) and its implications for studies of dog cognition' *Animal Cognition* 11(3):553-556 (https://doi.org/10.1007/s10071-007-0128-x)

Kelly S 2019 (12 Jan) 'Contrafeeloading: Why animals may prefer to work for food' *Shay's Dog Blog* (https://shaysdogblog.com/contrafreeloading-why-animals-may-prefer-to-work-for-food/)

Kirchhofer KC, Zimmermann F, Kaminski J, Tomasello M 2012 'Dogs (*Canis familiaris*), but not chimpanzees (*Pan troglodytes*), understand imperative pointing' *PLOS ONE* 7(2):e30913 (https://doi.org/10.1371/journal.pone.0030913)

Kujala MV 2017 'Canine emotions as seen through human social cognition' *Animal Sentience* 2(14):1-35 (https://animalstudiesrepository.org/cgi/viewcontent.cgi?article=1114&context=animsent)

Lakatos G, Gácsi M, Topál J, Miklósi A 2012 'Comprehension and utilisation of pointing gestures and gazing in dog-human communication in relatively complex situations' *Animal Cognition* 15:201-213 (https://doi.org/10.1007/s10071-011-0446-x)

London KB 2017 (Nov) 'Adolescent dogs go through fear periods' *Bark: The Dog Culture Magazine* (https://thebark.com/content/adolescent-dogs-go-through-fear-periods)

London KB 2019 (Feb) 'Take your dog on a sniffari' *Bark: The Dog Culture Magazine* (https://thebark.com/content/take-your-dog-sniffari)

Love is Respect n.d. 'What is a healthy relationship?' *Loveisrespect.org* (www.loveisrespect.org/healthy-relationships/)

Makowska IJ 2018 'Review of dog training methods: Welfare, learning ability, and current standards' *BC SPCA: Vancouver, Canada* (https://spca.bc.ca/wp-content/uploads/dog-training-methods-review.pdf)

Martin AL 2017 'The development and expression of canine emotion: Commentary on Kujala on *Canine Emotions*' *Animal Sentience* 2(14):1-3 (https://animalstudiesrepository.org/cgi/viewcontent.cgi?article=1261&context=animsent)

Mattinson P 2018 (10 March) 'The evidence for positive reinforcement training in dogs' *The Happy Puppy Site* (https://thehappypuppysite.com/the-evidence-for-positive-reinforcement-training-in-dogs/)

McKie R 2010 (27 June) 'Chimps with everything: Jane Goodall's 50 years in the jungle' *The Guardian* (https://www.theguardian.com/science/2010/jun/27/jane-goodall-chimps-africa-interview)

Miklósi A 2018 *The dog: A natural history* Ivy Press: London, UK (https://doi.org/10.23943/9781400889990)

Milikan D n.d. 'Defining, determining and maintain best practices within our force free organization' *Pet Professional Guild Australia* website (https://www.ppgaustralia.net.au/PPGBestPractices)

Mitchell T 2017 *How to be a concept trainer* First Stone Publishing: UK

National Dog Trainers Federation n.d. 'General Information' *NDTF* website (https://www.ndtf.net.au/wp-content/cache/all/general-information//index.html)

Nixon R 2012 (9 July) 'Adolescent angst: 5 facts about the teen brain' *LiveScience.com* (https://www.livescience.com/21461-teen-brain-adolescence-facts.html)

Patel C 2018 (23 Jan) 'Chirag Patel – Domesticated manners (the bucket game)' *Animal Training Academy podcast* (https://www.animaltrainingacademy.com/podcast/training-tidbits/chirag-patel/)

References

Pet Professional Guild n.d. 'Member search' *Pet Professional Guild* website (https://www.ppgaustralia.net.au/Member-Search)

Prato-Previde E and Marshall-Pescini S 2014 'Social looking in the domestic dog' (pg 101-132) In: A Horowitz (ed.) *Domestic dog cognition and behaviour: The scientific study of* Canis familiaris Springer: New York, NY (https://doi.org/10.1007/978-3-642-53994-7_5)

Riedel J, Shumann K, Kaminski J, Call J, Tomasello M 2008 'The early ontogeny of human-dog communication' *Animal Behaviour* 75(30):1003-1014 (https://doi.org/10.1016/j.anbehav.2007.08.010)

Reisner I 2014 (Nov/Dec) 'Moving beyond "leader of the pack": Changing dog behaviour using science instead of myth' *Today's Veterinary Practice* (https://todaysveterinarypractice.com/on-your-best-behavior-moving-beyond-leader-of-the-pack/)

Reusche S 2017 (16 Feb) 'Understanding dog-dog sociability' *Paws Ability blog* (https://paws4udogs.wordpress.com/2017/02/16/understanding-dog-dog-sociability/)

Safina C 2015 *Beyond words: What animals think and feel* Henry Hold and Company, LLC: New York, NY

Sapolsky RM 2003 'Stress and plasticity in the limbic system' *Neurochemical Research* 28(11):1735-1742 (https://doi.org/10.1023/A:1026021307833)

Schipper LL, Vinke CM, Schilder MBH, Spruijt BM 2008 'The effect of feeding enrichment toys on the behaviour of kennelled dogs (*Canis familiaris*)' *Applied Animal Behaviour Science* 114(1-2):182-195 (https://doi.org/10.1016/j.applanim.2008.01.001)

Sdao K 2012 *Plenty in life is free: Reflections on dogs, training and finding grace* Dogwise Publishing: Wenatchee, WA

Seligman MEP and Peterson C 2001 'Learned helplessness' (pg 8583-8586) *International Encyclopedia of the Social & Behavioral Sciences* Elsevier: Oxford, UK (https://doi.org/10.1016/B0-08-043076-7/00378-8)

Shore ER, Douglas DK, Riley ML 2005 'What's in it for the companion animal? Pet attachment and college students' behaviors towards pets' *Journal of Applied Animal Welfare Science* 8(1):1-11 (https://doi.org/10.1207/s15327604jaws0801_1)

Starling MJ, Branson N, Thomson PC, McGreevy PD 2013 'Age, sex and reproduction status affect boldness in dogs' *The Veterinary Journal* 197(3):868-872 (https://doi.org/10.1016/j.tvjl.2013.05.019)

Todd Z 2012 (4 July) 'Positive reinforcement and dog training' *Companion Animal Psychology* (https://www.companionanimalpsychology.com/2012/07/positive-reinforcement-and-dog-training.html)

Todd Z 2016 (14 Dec) 'How to choose a dog trainer' *Companion Animal Psychology* (https://www.companionanimalpsychology.com/2016/12/how-to-choose-dog-trainer.html)

Todd Z 2017 (1 Feb) 'What is positive reinforcement in dog training?' *Companion Animal Psychology* (https://www.companionanimalpsychology.com/2017/02/what-is-positive-reinforcement-in-dog.html)

Todd Z 2020 (15 Jan) 'Interview with Clive Wynne about *Dog Is Love*' *Companion Animal Psychology* (https://www.companionanimalpsychology.com/2020/01/interview-with-clive-wynne-about-dog-is.html)

Transport Accident Commission 2019 (viewed Jan 2020) 'Young drivers' Victorian government website (https://www.tac.vic.gov.au/road-safety/tac-campaigns/young-drivers)

Westlund K 2019 (22 March) 'Animal trainers: Take emotions into consideration!' *Illis Animal Behaviour Consulting* (https://karolinawestlund.com/en/animal-trainers-take-animal-emotions-into-consideration/)

Ziv G 2017 'The effects of using aversive training methods in dogs—A review' *Journal of Veterinary Behavior* 19:50-60 (https://doi.org/10.1016/j.jveb.2017.02.004)

Index

Index

Index

extinction burst 110
extinction of behaviours 110
eye drops 155

F

fear
  and reassurance 100
  and stress 44
  and undesirable behaviours 54, 88
  as a primary emotion 39
  associations 92
  car trips 65
  children on bikes 121
  counter-conditioning 121
  flooding 100
  phases 14
fear-free vet 80, 151, 154
flashbulb memories. *See* one-event
    learning
flooding 100
food
  and respondent conditioning 40,
    120
  and teeth 150
  as enrichment. *See* enrichment,
    nutritional
  chews 88, 89, 137, 139
  diversity 108
  toss game 133
foundation behaviours 128
four quadrants 50, 52
friends. *See* play dates and dog
    friends

G

Goodog Positive Dog Training 117,
    167
go-to-mat 45, 96, 125, 137
grooming. *See* brushing and
    grooming
guardians, why called a 23
guilty look 40

H

hand-touch 127, 128
happy dogs, signs of 31, 83, 104
head halters 145
head-rest 152, 154
head-turn 131
human, why called a 23
humping 46
husbandry
  and consent 32, 34
  brushing and grooming 157
  cleaning teeth 89, 149
  ear/eye drops 155
  head-rest 152
  muzzle training 157
  nail trimming 154
  step-on 152
  taking pills 156
  vets 150, 157
  why teach 136, 149

I

impulse control 7, 8, 10, 86, 129
independence training 67
inside access
  and barking 93, 94
  and being part of a social group 20
  importance of 24, 25, 93

J

jackpots 134
jealousy 41
job, dog. *See* enrichment,
    occupational
jumping

Index

Index

V

vets
  and crate-training 139
  Australian Veterinary Association
      49
  fear-free 80, 151, 154
  head-rest 152
  socialisation 80, 150
  step-on 152
  stress and fear 150, 157

W

watch-me 127, 128
weave 148
welfare, animal 37, 47, 53
wolf studies 21

Endnotes

1   Berns and Cook 2016
2   Berns 2016
3   Berns and Cook 2016
4   Kaminski et al. 2019; Lakatos et al. 2012; Prato-Previde and Marshall-Pescini 2014; Hare and Tomasello 2005; Riedel et al. 2008; Kirchhofer et al. 2012
5   Frederick 2019
6   Edmonds 2008
7   Transport Accident Commission 2019
8   Edmonds 2008
9   Nixon 2012
10   Transport Accident Commission 2019
11   Starling et al. 2013
12   Reusche 2017
13   London 2017
14   Haraway 2003 (pg 34-35)
15   Haraway 2003 (pg 96)
16   Miklósi 2018 (pg 6)
17   Safina 2015 (pg 410)
18   Arnold 2016
19   Mitchell 2017
20   Love is Respect n.d.
21   Horowitz 2009a (pg 57)
22   Reisner 2014
23   Carlisle-Frank and Frank 2006
24   Shore et al. 2005
25   Arnold 2016
26   Horowitz 2009a (pg 26)
27   Horowitz 2009a (pg 271)
28   Check out her website at https://www.susangarrett.com/
29   Garrett n.d.
30   Patel 2018
31   Bekoff 2019b
32   Kujala 2017
33   Westlund 2019
34   Cook 2017
35   Berns et al. 2015

Endnotes

36 Horowitz 2009b
37 Horowitz 2009b (pg 451)
38 Kujala 2017
39 Brucks et al. 2016
40 Harris and Prouvost 2014
41 Kujala 2017 (pg 14)
42 Burghardt 2007
43 Kujala 2017
44 Martin 2017
45 Dahl 2016
46 Safina 2015
47 Bekoff 2008
48 de Waal 2017
49 Joëls et al. 2006; Bangasser and Shors 2010
50 Sapolsky 2003
51 Sapolsky 2003
52 quoted in McKie 2010
53 Ziv 2017; Makowska 2018
54 Todd 2017; Mattinson 2018; Farricelli 2016; Bekoff 2019a
55 Todd 2012
56 Milikan n.d.
57 Delta Institute n.d.(a)
58 Australian Veterinary Association n.d.
59 Association of Pet Dog Trainers Australian Inc. n.d.(a)
60 National Dog Trainers Federation n.d.
61 American Heritage Dictionary of the English Language 2016
62 Anderson 2015, 2019; Farricelli 2016
63 Seligman and Peterson 2001
64 Ziv 2017
65 Todd 2020
66 check out www.puppyculture.com
67 www.calmsound.com is just one example
68 Dog Knowledge 2018; see also http://www.dogknowledge.co.uk/
69 https://fearfreepets.com/
70 Schipper et al. 2008
71 Ginman 2013
72 Balance Behaviour n.d.
73 Garvey et al. 2016
74 Herron et al. 2014

75   Schipper et al. 2008
76   De Rosa 2018
77   London 2019
78   Cattet 2013
79   Kelly 2019
80   Kaulfuß and Mills 2008
81   Bender and Strong 2019
82   Sdao 2012
83   Horowitz 2009a (pg 256)
84   Hunter 2016
85   Goodog YouTube Channel (https://www.youtube.com/user/TheGoodogchannel)
86   Goodog channel 2016c
87   Goodog channel 2016a
88   Cherry 2019
89   Makowska 2018
90   https://fearfreepets.com/
91   Goodog channel 2016b
92   Goodog Positive Dog Training 2017
93   https://muzzleupproject.com/
94   Pet Professional Guild n.d.
95   Delta Institute n.d.(b)
96   Association of Pet Dog Trainers Australia Inc. n.d.(b)
97   Todd 2016